Gifts from

Soups, Chilis & More

Memorable Gift Giving

Create an unforgettable gift for your friends and family by giving them a homemade gift jar filled with ingredients to make delicious soups, chilis, sides and snacks. Fill jars as directed and add your personal decorating touch. The result—a beautiful gift that will make a lasting impression. Since most of the ingredients are premeasured and in the jar, recipe preparation is easier and more fun.

Keep the following tips in mind when preparing your gift jars.

- Always use a food-safe jar or container with an airtight lid.

- Make sure the jar or container is completely dry before filling it with ingredients.

- Use the jar size called for in the recipe.

- Measure all the ingredients accurately.

- For ease in filling, use a canning funnel and a ¼-cup dry measuring cup.

- For a more attractive jar, follow the recipe as directed.

- Fill several jars at once for a make-ahead gift that can be stored until needed.

- After the jar is filled, make sure to replace the lid securely. Then, tear out the corresponding gift tag from the book with the recipe and preparation instructions. Cover the top of the jar with a 9- or 10-inch circle of fabric. Tie the fabric and the gift tag onto the jar with raffia, ribbon, satin cord, string, yarn or lace.

Italian Tomato and Pasta Soup Mix

2½ cups farfalle (bow tie) or rotini pasta
2 tablespoons dried vegetable flakes
1 tablespoon dried minced onion
1 teaspoon sugar
1 teaspoon chicken bouillon granules
1 teaspoon Italian herb seasoning
½ teaspoon dried minced garlic
¼ teaspoon black pepper
½ cup grated Parmesan cheese

1. Place pasta in 1-quart food storage jar with tight-fitting lid. Add vegetable flakes, onion, sugar, bouillon granules, Italian seasoning, garlic and pepper. Shake jar to mix seasoning. Place Parmesan cheese in small food storage bag. Close with twist tie and cut off top of bag. Place bag on top of pasta. Close jar.

2. Cover top of jar with fabric; attach gift tag with raffia or ribbon.

Makes one 1-quart jar

Italian Tomato and Pasta Soup

1 jar Italian Tomato and Pasta Soup Mix
5 cups water
1 can (28 ounces) crushed tomatoes
½ package (10 ounces) frozen chopped spinach, thawed
4 to 6 slices crisp-cooked bacon, crumbled

1. Remove cheese packet from jar; set aside.

2. Combine water and remaining contents of jar in large saucepan. Bring to a boil and boil 10 to 12 minutes. Stir in tomatoes, spinach and bacon. Reduce heat; simmer 10 to 12 minutes or until pasta is tender. Serve with Parmesan cheese.   *Makes 4 to 5 servings*

Variation: Substitute 2 to 3 cups chopped fresh spinach, rinsed and stemmed for frozen spinach.

Italian Tomato and Pasta Soup

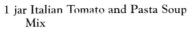

1 jar Italian Tomato and Pasta Soup
  Mix
5 cups water
1 can (28 ounces) crushed tomatoes

½ package (10 ounces) frozen chopped
  spinach, thawed
4 to 6 slices crisp-cooked bacon,
  crumbled

1. Remove cheese packet from jar; set aside.

2. Combine water and remaining contents of jar in large saucepan. Bring to a boil and boil 10 to 12 minutes. Stir in tomatoes, spinach and bacon. Reduce heat; simmer 10 to 12 minutes or until pasta is tender. Serve with Parmesan cheese.   *Makes 4 to 5 servings*

Variation: Substitute 2 to 3 cups chopped fresh spinach, rinsed and stemmed for frozen spinach.

Italian Tomato and Pasta Soup

1 jar Italian Tomato and Pasta Soup
  Mix
5 cups water
1 can (28 ounces) crushed tomatoes

½ package (10 ounces) frozen chopped
  spinach, thawed
4 to 6 slices crisp-cooked bacon,
  crumbled

1. Remove cheese packet from jar; set aside.

2. Combine water and remaining contents of jar in large saucepan. Bring to a boil and boil 10 to 12 minutes. Stir in tomatoes, spinach and bacon. Reduce heat; simmer 10 to 12 minutes or until pasta is tender. Serve with Parmesan cheese.   *Makes 4 to 5 servings*

Variation: Substitute 2 to 3 cups chopped fresh spinach, rinsed and stemmed for frozen spinach.

Italian Tomato and Pasta Soup

1 jar Italian Tomato and Pasta Soup
  Mix
5 cups water
1 can (28 ounces) crushed tomatoes

½ package (10 ounces) frozen chopped
  spinach, thawed
4 to 6 slices crisp-cooked bacon,
  crumbled

1. Remove cheese packet from jar; set aside.

2. Combine water and remaining contents of jar in large saucepan. Bring to a boil and boil 10 to 12 minutes. Stir in tomatoes, spinach and bacon. Reduce heat; simmer 10 to 12 minutes or until pasta is tender. Serve with Parmesan cheese.   *Makes 4 to 5 servings*

Variation: Substitute 2 to 3 cups chopped fresh spinach, rinsed and stemmed for frozen spinach.

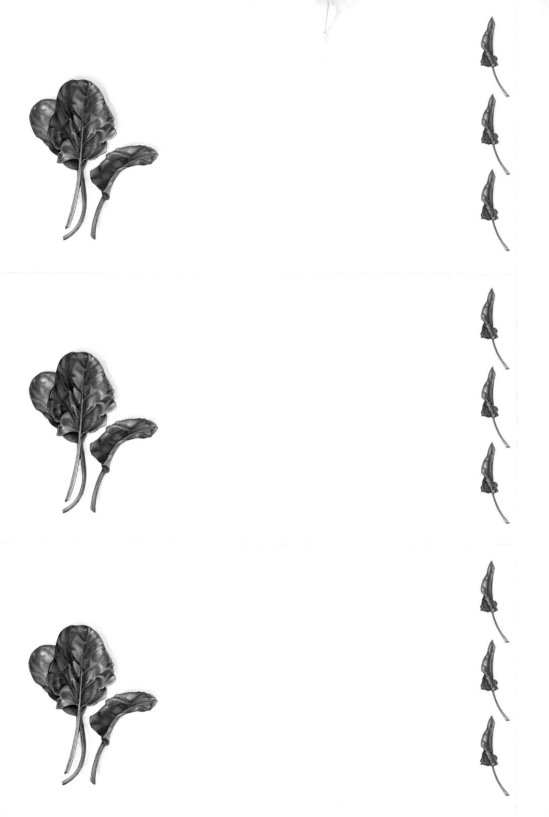

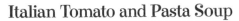

Italian Tomato and Pasta Soup

1 jar Italian Tomato and Pasta Soup
    Mix
5 cups water
1 can (28 ounces) crushed tomatoes

½ package (10 ounces) frozen chopped
    spinach, thawed
4 to 6 slices crisp-cooked bacon,
    crumbled

1. Remove cheese packet from jar; set aside.

2. Combine water and remaining contents of jar in large saucepan. Bring to a boil and boil
10 to 12 minutes. Stir in tomatoes, spinach and bacon. Reduce heat; simmer 10 to 12
minutes or until pasta is tender. Serve with Parmesan cheese.   *Makes 4 to 5 servings*

Variation: Substitute 2 to 3 cups chopped fresh spinach, rinsed and stemmed for frozen
spinach.

Italian Tomato and Pasta Soup

1 jar Italian Tomato and Pasta Soup
    Mix
5 cups water
1 can (28 ounces) crushed tomatoes

½ package (10 ounces) frozen chopped
    spinach, thawed
4 to 6 slices crisp-cooked bacon,
    crumbled

1. Remove cheese packet from jar; set aside.

2. Combine water and remaining contents of jar in large saucepan. Bring to a boil and boil
10 to 12 minutes. Stir in tomatoes, spinach and bacon. Reduce heat; simmer 10 to 12
minutes or until pasta is tender. Serve with Parmesan cheese.   *Makes 4 to 5 servings*

Variation: Substitute 2 to 3 cups chopped fresh spinach, rinsed and stemmed for frozen
spinach.

Italian Tomato and Pasta Soup

1 jar Italian Tomato and Pasta Soup
    Mix
5 cups water
1 can (28 ounces) crushed tomatoes

½ package (10 ounces) frozen chopped
    spinach, thawed
4 to 6 slices crisp-cooked bacon,
    crumbled

1. Remove cheese packet from jar; set aside.

2. Combine water and remaining contents of jar in large saucepan. Bring to a boil and boil
10 to 12 minutes. Stir in tomatoes, spinach and bacon. Reduce heat; simmer 10 to 12
minutes or until pasta is tender. Serve with Parmesan cheese.   *Makes 4 to 5 servings*

Variation: Substitute 2 to 3 cups chopped fresh spinach, rinsed and stemmed for frozen
spinach.

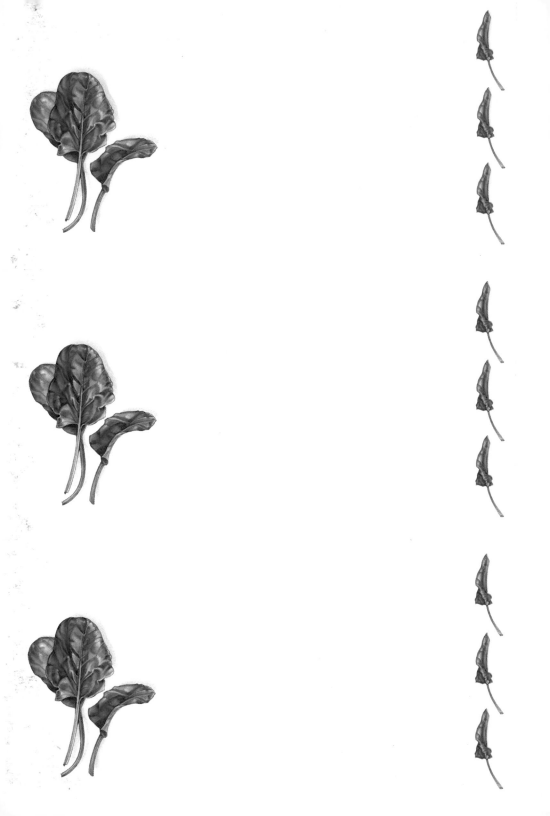

Hearty Lentil & Barley Soup Mix

¾ cup brown or red lentils
¼ cup sun-dried tomato halves, cut into pieces
2 tablespoons dried vegetable flakes
1 tablespoon dried minced onion
2 teaspoons chicken bouillon granules
1 teaspoon dried oregano leaves
½ teaspoon dried minced garlic
½ teaspoon black pepper
⅛ teaspoon red pepper flakes (optional)
½ cup uncooked medium pearled barley

1. Layer lentils, sun-dried tomatoes, vegetable flakes, onion, bouillon granules, oregano, garlic, black pepper, red pepper flakes, if desired, and barley in 1-pint food storage jar with tight-fitting lid. Close jar.

2. Cover top of jar with fabric; attach gift tag with raffia or ribbon.

Makes one 1-pint jar

Hearty Lentil & Barley Soup

1 jar Hearty Lentil & Barley Soup Mix
5 to 6 cups water
1 can (14½ ounces) diced tomatoes with green pepper, celery
    and onion, undrained
8 ounces smoked sausage, cut into ½-inch slices
    Lemon pepper

Place contents of jar, water, tomatoes and sausage in slow cooker. Stir; cover and cook on LOW 6 to 8 hours. Add additional water, ½ cup at a time, if needed to reach desired consistency. Season to taste with lemon pepper. *Makes 10 to 12 servings*

Conventional Method: Simmer ingredients in Dutch oven, partially covered, 1 to 1½ hours or until lentils and barley are tender.

Hearty Lentil & Barley Soup

1 jar Hearty Lentil & Barley Soup
Mix
5 to 6 cups water
1 can (14½ ounces) diced tomatoes
with green pepper, celery and
onion, undrained

8 ounces smoked sausage, cut into
½-inch slices
Lemon pepper

Place contents of jar, water, tomatoes and sausage in slow cooker. Stir; cover and cook on LOW 6 to 8 hours. Add additional water, ½ cup at a time, if needed to reach desired consistency. Season to taste with lemon pepper. *Makes 10 to 12 servings*

Conventional Method: Simmer ingredients in Dutch oven, partially covered, 1 to 1½ hours or until lentils and barley are tender.

Hearty Lentil & Barley Soup

1 jar Hearty Lentil & Barley Soup
Mix
5 to 6 cups water
1 can (14½ ounces) diced tomatoes
with green pepper, celery and
onion, undrained

8 ounces smoked sausage, cut into
½-inch slices
Lemon pepper

Place contents of jar, water, tomatoes and sausage in slow cooker. Stir; cover and cook on LOW 6 to 8 hours. Add additional water, ½ cup at a time, if needed to reach desired consistency. Season to taste with lemon pepper. *Makes 10 to 12 servings*

Conventional Method: Simmer ingredients in Dutch oven, partially covered, 1 to 1½ hours or until lentils and barley are tender.

Hearty Lentil & Barley Soup

1 jar Hearty Lentil & Barley Soup
Mix
5 to 6 cups water
1 can (14½ ounces) diced tomatoes
with green pepper, celery and
onion, undrained

8 ounces smoked sausage, cut into
½-inch slices
Lemon pepper

Place contents of jar, water, tomatoes and sausage in slow cooker. Stir; cover and cook on LOW 6 to 8 hours. Add additional water, ½ cup at a time, if needed to reach desired consistency. Season to taste with lemon pepper. *Makes 10 to 12 servings*

Conventional Method: Simmer ingredients in Dutch oven, partially covered, 1 to 1½ hours or until lentils and barley are tender.

Hearty Lentil & Barley Soup

1 jar Hearty Lentil & Barley Soup
   Mix
5 to 6 cups water
1 can (14½ ounces) diced tomatoes
   with green pepper, celery and
   onion, undrained

8 ounces smoked sausage, cut into
   ½-inch slices
Lemon pepper

Place contents of jar, water, tomatoes and sausage in slow cooker. Stir; cover and cook on
LOW 6 to 8 hours. Add additional water, ½ cup at a time, if needed to reach desired
consistency. Season to taste with lemon pepper.   *Makes 10 to 12 servings*

Conventional Method: Simmer ingredients in Dutch oven, partially covered, 1 to 1½
hours or until lentils and barley are tender.

Hearty Lentil & Barley Soup

1 jar Hearty Lentil & Barley Soup
   Mix
5 to 6 cups water
1 can (14½ ounces) diced tomatoes
   with green pepper, celery and
   onion, undrained

8 ounces smoked sausage, cut into
   ½-inch slices
Lemon pepper

Place contents of jar, water, tomatoes and sausage in slow cooker. Stir; cover and cook on
LOW 6 to 8 hours. Add additional water, ½ cup at a time, if needed to reach desired
consistency. Season to taste with lemon pepper.   *Makes 10 to 12 servings*

Conventional Method: Simmer ingredients in Dutch oven, partially covered, 1 to 1½
hours or until lentils and barley are tender.

Hearty Lentil & Barley Soup

1 jar Hearty Lentil & Barley Soup
   Mix
5 to 6 cups water
1 can (14½ ounces) diced tomatoes
   with green pepper, celery and
   onion, undrained

8 ounces smoked sausage, cut into
   ½-inch slices
Lemon pepper

Place contents of jar, water, tomatoes and sausage in slow cooker. Stir; cover and cook on
LOW 6 to 8 hours. Add additional water, ½ cup at a time, if needed to reach desired
consistency. Season to taste with lemon pepper.   *Makes 10 to 12 servings*

Conventional Method: Simmer ingredients in Dutch oven, partially covered, 1 to 1½
hours or until lentils and barley are tender.

Creamy Potato-Cheese Soup Mix

2 cups instant mashed potato flakes
1 package (about 1¼ ounces) dried Cheddar cheese sauce mix
1 tablespoon dried chives
1 teaspoon chicken bouillon granules
½ teaspoon dry mustard
¼ teaspoon white pepper
1½ cups herbed croutons

1. Layer 1 cup potato flakes, cheese sauce mix, chives, bouillon granules, dry mustard, white pepper and remaining 1 cup potato flakes in 1-quart food storage jar with tight-fitting lid. Place croutons in small food storage bag. Close with twist tie and cut off top of bag. Place on top of potato flakes. Close jar.

2. Cover top of jar with fabric; attach gift tag with raffia or ribbon.

Makes one 1-quart jar

Creamy Potato-Cheese Soup

1 jar Creamy Potato-Cheese Soup Mix
3 cups water
2 cups milk
½ to 1 cup sour cream or plain yogurt
   Hot pepper sauce (optional)

1. Carefully remove packet of croutons from jar; set aside.

2. Bring water and milk to a boil in large saucepan over high heat. Whisk in remaining contents of jar. Reduce heat; simmer 5 minutes, stirring constantly. Whisk in sour cream. Add additional water or milk, ½ cup at a time, to reach desired consistency. Season with hot pepper sauce, if desired. Serve with croutons.

Makes 5 to 6 servings

Variations: Stir in 2 cups cooked broccoli florets or 2 cups cubed cooked ham. Heat through.

Creamy Potato-Cheese Soup

1 jar Creamy Potato-Cheese Soup Mix
3 cups water
2 cups milk

½ to 1 cup sour cream or plain yogurt
Hot pepper sauce (optional)

1. Carefully remove packet of croutons from jar; set aside.

2. Bring water and milk to a boil in large saucepan over high heat. Whisk in remaining contents of jar. Reduce heat; simmer 5 minutes, stirring constantly. Whisk in sour cream. Add additional water or milk, ½ cup at a time, to reach desired consistency. Season with hot pepper sauce, if desired. Serve with croutons. *Makes 5 to 6 servings*

Variations: Stir in 2 cups cooked broccoli florets or 2 cups cubed cooked ham. Heat through.

Creamy Potato-Cheese Soup

1 jar Creamy Potato-Cheese Soup Mix
3 cups water
2 cups milk

½ to 1 cup sour cream or plain yogurt
Hot pepper sauce (optional)

1. Carefully remove packet of croutons from jar; set aside.

2. Bring water and milk to a boil in large saucepan over high heat. Whisk in remaining contents of jar. Reduce heat; simmer 5 minutes, stirring constantly. Whisk in sour cream. Add additional water or milk, ½ cup at a time, to reach desired consistency. Season with hot pepper sauce, if desired. Serve with croutons. *Makes 5 to 6 servings*

Variations: Stir in 2 cups cooked broccoli florets or 2 cups cubed cooked ham. Heat through.

Creamy Potato-Cheese Soup

1 jar Creamy Potato-Cheese Soup Mix
3 cups water
2 cups milk

½ to 1 cup sour cream or plain yogurt
Hot pepper sauce (optional)

1. Carefully remove packet of croutons from jar; set aside.

2. Bring water and milk to a boil in large saucepan over high heat. Whisk in remaining contents of jar. Reduce heat; simmer 5 minutes, stirring constantly. Whisk in sour cream. Add additional water or milk, ½ cup at a time, to reach desired consistency. Season with hot pepper sauce, if desired. Serve with croutons. *Makes 5 to 6 servings*

Variations: Stir in 2 cups cooked broccoli florets or 2 cups cubed cooked ham. Heat through.

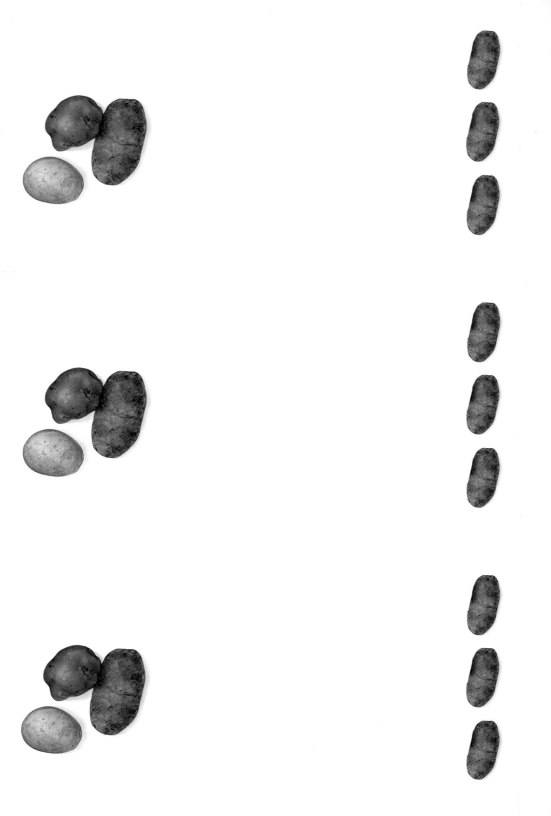

Creamy Potato-Cheese Soup

1 jar Creamy Potato-Cheese Soup Mix
3 cups water
2 cups milk

½ to 1 cup sour cream or plain yogurt
Hot pepper sauce (optional)

1. Carefully remove packet of croutons from jar; set aside.

2. Bring water and milk to a boil in large saucepan over high heat. Whisk in remaining contents of jar. Reduce heat; simmer 5 minutes, stirring constantly. Whisk in sour cream. Add additional water or milk, ½ cup at a time, to reach desired consistency. Season with hot pepper sauce, if desired. Serve with croutons.   *Makes 5 to 6 servings*

Variations: Stir in 2 cups cooked broccoli florets or 2 cups cubed cooked ham. Heat through.

Creamy Potato-Cheese Soup

1 jar Creamy Potato-Cheese Soup Mix
3 cups water
2 cups milk

½ to 1 cup sour cream or plain yogurt
Hot pepper sauce (optional)

1. Carefully remove packet of croutons from jar; set aside.

2. Bring water and milk to a boil in large saucepan over high heat. Whisk in remaining contents of jar. Reduce heat; simmer 5 minutes, stirring constantly. Whisk in sour cream. Add additional water or milk, ½ cup at a time, to reach desired consistency. Season with hot pepper sauce, if desired. Serve with croutons.   *Makes 5 to 6 servings*

Variations: Stir in 2 cups cooked broccoli florets or 2 cups cubed cooked ham. Heat through.

Creamy Potato-Cheese Soup

1 jar Creamy Potato-Cheese Soup Mix
3 cups water
2 cups milk

½ to 1 cup sour cream or plain yogurt
Hot pepper sauce (optional)

1. Carefully remove packet of croutons from jar; set aside.

2. Bring water and milk to a boil in large saucepan over high heat. Whisk in remaining contents of jar. Reduce heat; simmer 5 minutes, stirring constantly. Whisk in sour cream. Add additional water or milk, ½ cup at a time, to reach desired consistency. Season with hot pepper sauce, if desired. Serve with croutons.   *Makes 5 to 6 servings*

Variations: Stir in 2 cups cooked broccoli florets or 2 cups cubed cooked ham. Heat through.

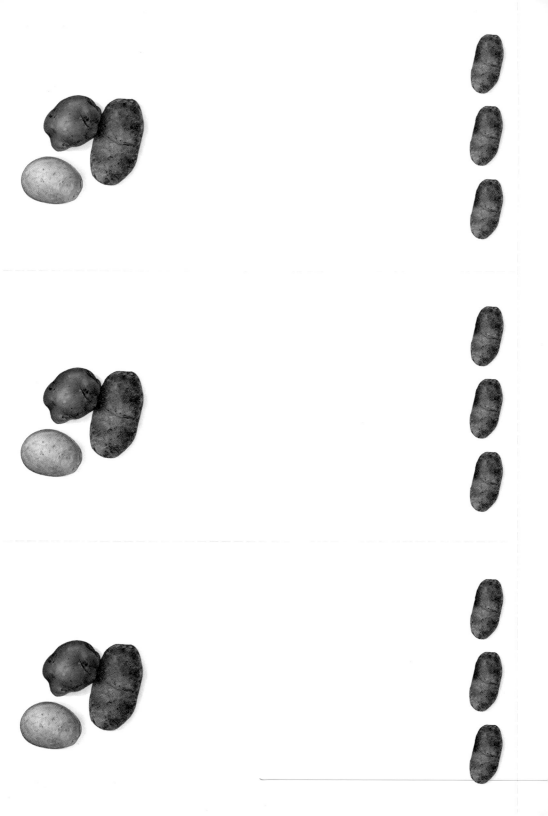

Hoppin' John Soup Mix

1 cup dried black-eyed peas
1 tablespoon dried minced onion
1 tablespoon dried vegetable flakes
1 chicken bouillon cube, unwrapped
1 teaspoon dried minced garlic
1 teaspoon dried thyme leaves
½ teaspoon ground cumin
¼ teaspoon black pepper
⅛ teaspoon ground red pepper
1 boil-in-bag white rice

1. Place black-eyed peas in 1-pint food storage jar with tight-fitting lid. Place onion, vegetable flakes, bouillon cube, garlic, thyme, cumin, black pepper and red pepper into small food storage bag. Close with twist tie and cut off the top. Place on top of peas; add bag of rice. Close jar.

2. Cover top of jar with fabric; attach gift tag with raffia or ribbon.

Makes one 1-pint jar

Hoppin' John Soup

1 jar Hoppin' John Soup Mix
2 to 3 cups water
1 can (14½ ounces) tomatoes with green chilies, undrained
4 slices crisp-cooked bacon, crumbled *or* 1 smoked ham hock
  Lemon pepper or hot pepper sauce
  Chopped parsley (optional)

1. Remove rice and seasoning packet from jar; set aside. Place beans in large bowl; cover with water. Soak 6 to 8 hours or overnight. (To quick soak beans, place beans in large saucepan; cover with water. Bring to a boil over high heat. Boil 2 minutes. Remove from heat; let soak, covered, 1 hour.) Drain beans; discard water.

2. Place soaked beans, water, tomatoes, bacon and contents of seasoning packet into large saucepan. Bring to a boil over high heat. Cover; reduce heat and simmer 1½ to 2 hours or until beans are tender. Mash beans slightly with potato masher. Season with lemon pepper. Submerge bag of rice in boiling salted water; boil 10 minutes. Drain rice; mix with parsley, if desired. Serve soup with rice.   *Makes 4 to 6 servings*

Hoppin' John Soup

1 jar Hoppin' John Soup Mix
2 to 3 cups water
1 can (14½ ounces) tomatoes with
green chilies, undrained

4 slices crisp-cooked bacon, crumbled
or 1 smoked ham hock
Lemon pepper or hot pepper sauce
Chopped parsley (optional)

1. Remove rice and seasoning packet from jar; set aside. Place beans in bowl; cover with water. Soak 6 to 8 hours or overnight. (To quick soak beans, place beans in large saucepan; cover with water. Bring to a boil over high heat. Boil 2 minutes. Remove from heat; let soak, covered, 1 hour.) Drain beans; discard water.

2. Place soaked beans, water, tomatoes, bacon and contents of seasoning packet into large saucepan. Bring to a boil over high heat. Cover; reduce heat and simmer 1½ to 2 hours or until beans are tender. Mash beans slightly with potato masher. Season with lemon pepper. Submerge bag of rice in boiling salted water; boil 10 minutes. Drain rice; mix with parsley, if desired. Serve soup with rice.

Makes 10 to 12 servings

Hoppin' John Soup

1 jar Hoppin' John Soup Mix
2 to 3 cups water
1 can (14½ ounces) tomatoes with
green chilies, undrained

4 slices crisp-cooked bacon, crumbled
or 1 smoked ham hock
Lemon pepper or hot pepper sauce
Chopped parsley (optional)

1. Remove rice and seasoning packet from jar; set aside. Place beans in bowl; cover with water. Soak 6 to 8 hours or overnight. (To quick soak beans, place beans in large saucepan; cover with water. Bring to a boil over high heat. Boil 2 minutes. Remove from heat; let soak, covered, 1 hour.) Drain beans; discard water.

2. Place soaked beans, water, tomatoes, bacon and contents of seasoning packet into large saucepan. Bring to a boil over high heat. Cover; reduce heat and simmer 1½ to 2 hours or until beans are tender. Mash beans slightly with potato masher. Season with lemon pepper. Submerge bag of rice in boiling salted water; boil 10 minutes. Drain rice; mix with parsley, if desired. Serve soup with rice.

Makes 10 to 12 servings

Hoppin' John Soup

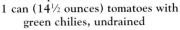

1 jar Hoppin' John Soup Mix
2 to 3 cups water
1 can (14½ ounces) tomatoes with
green chilies, undrained

4 slices crisp-cooked bacon, crumbled
or 1 smoked ham hock
Lemon pepper or hot pepper sauce
Chopped parsley (optional)

1. Remove rice and seasoning packet from jar; set aside. Place beans in bowl; cover with water. Soak 6 to 8 hours or overnight. (To quick soak beans, place beans in large saucepan; cover with water. Bring to a boil over high heat. Boil 2 minutes. Remove from heat; let soak, covered, 1 hour.) Drain beans; discard water.

2. Place soaked beans, water, tomatoes, bacon and contents of seasoning packet into large saucepan. Bring to a boil over high heat. Cover; reduce heat and simmer 1½ to 2 hours or until beans are tender. Mash beans slightly with potato masher. Season with lemon pepper. Submerge bag of rice in boiling salted water; boil 10 minutes. Drain rice; mix with parsley, if desired. Serve soup with rice.

Makes 10 to 12 servings

Hoppin' John Soup

1 jar Hoppin' John Soup Mix
2 to 3 cups water
1 can (14½ ounces) tomatoes with
   green chilies, undrained

4 slices crisp-cooked bacon, crumbled
   or 1 smoked ham hock
Lemon pepper or hot pepper sauce
Chopped parsley (optional)

1. Remove rice and seasoning packet from jar; set aside. Place beans in bowl; cover with water. Soak 6 to 8 hours or overnight. (To quick soak beans, place beans in large saucepan; cover with water. Bring to a boil over high heat. Boil 2 minutes. Remove from heat; let soak, covered, 1 hour.) Drain beans; discard water.

2. Place soaked beans, water, tomatoes, bacon and contents of seasoning packet into large saucepan. Bring to a boil over high heat. Cover; reduce heat and simmer 1½ to 2 hours or until beans are tender. Mash beans slightly with potato masher. Season with lemon pepper. Submerge bag of rice in boiling salted water; boil 10 minutes. Drain rice; mix with parsley, if desired. Serve soup with rice.
    Makes 10 to 12 servings

Hoppin' John Soup

1 jar Hoppin' John Soup Mix
2 to 3 cups water
1 can (14½ ounces) tomatoes with
   green chilies, undrained

4 slices crisp-cooked bacon, crumbled
   or 1 smoked ham hock
Lemon pepper or hot pepper sauce
Chopped parsley (optional)

1. Remove rice and seasoning packet from jar; set aside. Place beans in bowl; cover with water. Soak 6 to 8 hours or overnight. (To quick soak beans, place beans in large saucepan; cover with water. Bring to a boil over high heat. Boil 2 minutes. Remove from heat; let soak, covered, 1 hour.) Drain beans; discard water.

2. Place soaked beans, water, tomatoes, bacon and contents of seasoning packet into large saucepan. Bring to a boil over high heat. Cover; reduce heat and simmer 1½ to 2 hours or until beans are tender. Mash beans slightly with potato masher. Season with lemon pepper. Submerge bag of rice in boiling salted water; boil 10 minutes. Drain rice; mix with parsley, if desired. Serve soup with rice.
    Makes 10 to 12 servings

Hoppin' John Soup

1 jar Hoppin' John Soup Mix
2 to 3 cups water
1 can (14½ ounces) tomatoes with
   green chilies, undrained

4 slices crisp-cooked bacon, crumbled
   or 1 smoked ham hock
Lemon pepper or hot pepper sauce
Chopped parsley (optional)

1. Remove rice and seasoning packet from jar; set aside. Place beans in bowl; cover with water. Soak 6 to 8 hours or overnight. (To quick soak beans, place beans in large saucepan; cover with water. Bring to a boil over high heat. Boil 2 minutes. Remove from heat; let soak, covered, 1 hour.) Drain beans; discard water.

2. Place soaked beans, water, tomatoes, bacon and contents of seasoning packet into large saucepan. Bring to a boil over high heat. Cover; reduce heat and simmer 1½ to 2 hours or until beans are tender. Mash beans slightly with potato masher. Season with lemon pepper. Submerge bag of rice in boiling salted water; boil 10 minutes. Drain rice; mix with parsley, if desired. Serve soup with rice.
    Makes 10 to 12 servings

Home-Style Chicken & Rice Soup Mix

½ cup dried yellow split peas or wild rice

2 tablespoons dried minced onion

2 tablespoons dried vegetable flakes

2 teaspoons chicken bouillon granules

1 teaspoon dried thyme leaves

½ teaspoon minced garlic

½ teaspoon dried marjoram

½ teaspoon lemon pepper

1 cup uncooked brown rice

1 bay leaf

1. Layer split peas, onion, vegetable flakes, bouillon granules, thyme, garlic, marjoram, lemon pepper and rice in 1-pint food storage jar with tight-fitting lid. Slide bay leaf down side of jar. Close jar.

2. Cover top of jar with fabric; attach gift tag with raffia or ribbon.

Makes one 1-pint jar

Gift Idea: Assemble a gift basket with a jar of Home-Style Chicken and Rice Soup Mix, a can of tomato sauce and a package of muffin mix. Complete the basket with decorative soup bowls.

Home-Style Chicken & Rice Soup

1 jar Home-Style Chicken & Rice Soup Mix
6 to 7 cups water
1 can (8 ounces) tomato sauce
2 cups cubed cooked chicken
   Salt and pepper

1. Combine contents of jar, water and tomato sauce in Dutch oven. Bring to a boil over high heat. Cover; reduce heat and simmer 1 hour or until peas are tender.

2. Stir in chicken. Cook over low heat 10 to 15 minutes or until chicken is heated through. Remove and discard bay leaf. Season to taste. *Makes 10 to 12 servings*

Home-Style Chicken & Rice Soup

1 jar Home-Style Chicken & Rice
   Soup Mix
6 to 7 cups water

1 can (8 ounces) tomato sauce
2 cups cubed cooked chicken
Salt and pepper

1. Combine contents of jar, water and tomato sauce in Dutch oven. Bring to a boil over high heat. Cover; reduce heat and simmer 1 hour or until peas are tender.

2. Stir in chicken. Cook over low heat 10 to 15 minutes or until chicken is heated through. Remove and discard bay leaf. Season to taste. *Makes 10 to 12 servings*

Home-Style Chicken & Rice Soup

1 jar Home-Style Chicken & Rice
   Soup Mix
6 to 7 cups water

1 can (8 ounces) tomato sauce
2 cups cubed cooked chicken
Salt and pepper

1. Combine contents of jar, water and tomato sauce in Dutch oven. Bring to a boil over high heat. Cover; reduce heat and simmer 1 hour or until peas are tender.

2. Stir in chicken. Cook over low heat 10 to 15 minutes or until chicken is heated through. Remove and discard bay leaf. Season to taste. *Makes 10 to 12 servings*

Home-Style Chicken & Rice Soup

1 jar Home-Style Chicken & Rice
   Soup Mix
6 to 7 cups water

1 can (8 ounces) tomato sauce
2 cups cubed cooked chicken
Salt and pepper

1. Combine contents of jar, water and tomato sauce in Dutch oven. Bring to a boil over high heat. Cover; reduce heat and simmer 1 hour or until peas are tender.

2. Stir in chicken. Cook over low heat 10 to 15 minutes or until chicken is heated through. Remove and discard bay leaf. Season to taste. *Makes 10 to 12 servings*

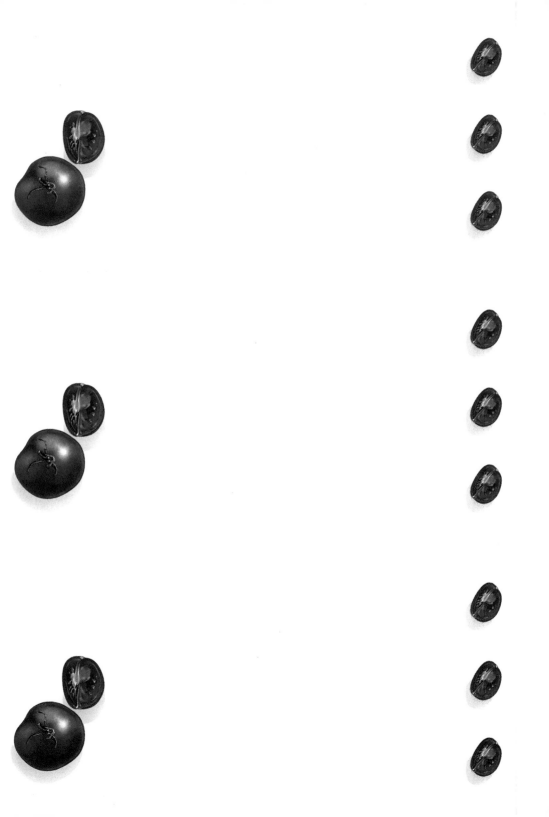

Home-Style Chicken & Rice Soup

1 jar Home-Style Chicken & Rice
   Soup Mix
6 to 7 cups water

1 can (8 ounces) tomato sauce
2 cups cubed cooked chicken
Salt and pepper

1. Combine contents of jar, water and tomato sauce in Dutch oven. Bring to a boil over high heat. Cover; reduce heat and simmer 1 hour or until peas are tender.

2. Stir in chicken. Cook over low heat 10 to 15 minutes or until chicken is heated through. Remove and discard bay leaf. Season to taste.   *Makes 10 to 12 servings*

Home-Style Chicken & Rice Soup

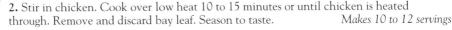

1 jar Home-Style Chicken & Rice
   Soup Mix
6 to 7 cups water

1 can (8 ounces) tomato sauce
2 cups cubed cooked chicken
Salt and pepper

1. Combine contents of jar, water and tomato sauce in Dutch oven. Bring to a boil over high heat. Cover; reduce heat and simmer 1 hour or until peas are tender.

2. Stir in chicken. Cook over low heat 10 to 15 minutes or until chicken is heated through. Remove and discard bay leaf. Season to taste.   *Makes 10 to 12 servings*

Home-Style Chicken & Rice Soup

1 jar Home-Style Chicken & Rice
   Soup Mix
6 to 7 cups water

1 can (8 ounces) tomato sauce
2 cups cubed cooked chicken
Salt and pepper

1. Combine contents of jar, water and tomato sauce in Dutch oven. Bring to a boil over high heat. Cover; reduce heat and simmer 1 hour or until peas are tender.

2. Stir in chicken. Cook over low heat 10 to 15 minutes or until chicken is heated through. Remove and discard bay leaf. Season to taste.   *Makes 10 to 12 servings*

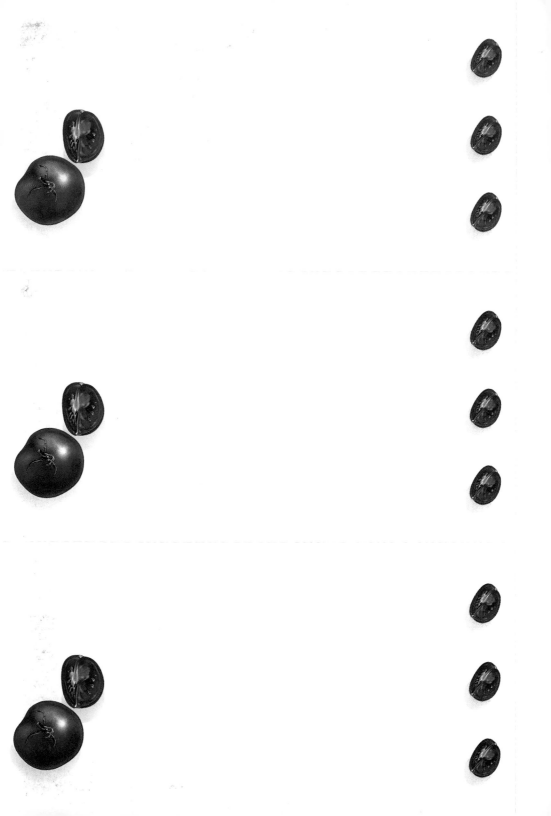

Country Six-Bean Soup Mix

½ cup dried red beans
½ cup dried navy beans
½ cup dried pinto beans
½ cup dried baby lima beans
½ cup dried kidney beans
½ cup dried Great Northern beans
2 bay leaves
2 tablespoons dried minced onion
1 tablespoon dried parsley flakes
2 teaspoons beef bouillon granules
1 teaspoon dried minced garlic
1 teaspoon dried thyme leaves
½ teaspoon dried oregano leaves
½ teaspoon black pepper
¼ teaspoon red pepper flakes

1. Layer red beans, navy beans, pinto beans, baby lima beans, kidney beans and Great Northern beans in 1-quart food storage jar with tight-fitting lid. Slide bay leaves down side of jar. Place onion, parsley, bouillon granules, garlic, thyme, oregano, black pepper and red pepper flakes in small food-storage bag. Close with twist tie; cut off top of bag. Place bag on top of beans. Close jar.

2. Cover top of jar with fabric; attach gift tag with raffia or ribbon.

Makes one 1-quart jar

Country Six-Bean Soup

1 jar Country Six-Bean Soup Mix
4 to 5 cups water
1 can (28 ounces) diced tomatoes with Italian seasonings
8 ounces smoked sausage links, sliced *or* 2 smoked ham hocks
   Hot pepper sauce or red wine vinegar (optional)

1. Remove seasoning packet and bay leaves; set aside.

2. Place beans in large bowl; cover with water. Soak 6 to 8 hours or overnight. (To quick soak beans, place beans in large saucepan; cover with water. Bring to a boil over high heat. Boil 2 minutes. Remove from heat; let soak, covered, 1 hour.) Drain beans; discard water.

3. Combine soaked beans, water, tomatoes, sausage, contents of seasoning packet and reserved bay leaves into Dutch oven. Bring to a boil over high heat. Cover; reduce heat and simmer 1½ to 2 hours or until beans are tender. Season to taste with hot pepper sauce, if desired.   *Makes 8 to 10 servings*

Note: For thicker consistency, mash beans slightly with potato masher.

Country Six-Bean Soup

1 jar Country-Six Bean Soup Mix
4 to 5 cups water
1 can (28 ounces) diced tomatoes
   with Italian seasonings

8 ounces smoked sausage links, sliced
   or smoked ham hocks
Hot pepper sauce or red wine
   vinegar (optional)

1. Remove seasoning packet and bay leaves; set aside.

2. Place beans in large bowl; cover with water. Soak 6 to 8 hours or overnight. (To quick soak beans, place beans in large saucepan; cover with water. Bring to a boil over high heat. Boil 2 minutes. Remove from heat; let soak, covered, 1 hour.) Drain beans; discard water.

3. Combine soaked beans, water, tomatoes, sausage, contents of seasoning packet and reserved bay leaves into Dutch oven. Bring to a boil over high heat. Cover; reduce heat and simmer 1½ to 2 hours or until beans are tender. Season to taste with hot pepper sauce, if desired. *Makes 8 to 10 servings*

Note: For thicker consistency, mash beans slightly with potato masher.

Country Six-Bean Soup

1 jar Country-Six Bean Soup Mix
4 to 5 cups water
1 can (28 ounces) diced tomatoes
   with Italian seasonings

8 ounces smoked sausage links, sliced
   or smoked ham hocks
Hot pepper sauce or red wine
   vinegar (optional)

1. Remove seasoning packet and bay leaves; set aside.

2. Place beans in large bowl; cover with water. Soak 6 to 8 hours or overnight. (To quick soak beans, place beans in large saucepan; cover with water. Bring to a boil over high heat. Boil 2 minutes. Remove from heat; let soak, covered, 1 hour.) Drain beans; discard water.

3. Combine soaked beans, water, tomatoes, sausage, contents of seasoning packet and reserved bay leaves into Dutch oven. Bring to a boil over high heat. Cover; reduce heat and simmer 1½ to 2 hours or until beans are tender. Season to taste with hot pepper sauce, if desired. *Makes 8 to 10 servings*

Note: For thicker consistency, mash beans slightly with potato masher.

Country Six-Bean Soup

1 jar Country-Six Bean Soup Mix
4 to 5 cups water
1 can (28 ounces) diced tomatoes
   with Italian seasonings

8 ounces smoked sausage links, sliced
   or smoked ham hocks
Hot pepper sauce or red wine
   vinegar (optional)

1. Remove seasoning packet and bay leaves; set aside.

2. Place beans in large bowl; cover with water. Soak 6 to 8 hours or overnight. (To quick soak beans, place beans in large saucepan; cover with water. Bring to a boil over high heat. Boil 2 minutes. Remove from heat; let soak, covered, 1 hour.) Drain beans; discard water.

3. Combine soaked beans, water, tomatoes, sausage, contents of seasoning packet and reserved bay leaves into Dutch oven. Bring to a boil over high heat. Cover; reduce heat and simmer 1½ to 2 hours or until beans are tender. Season to taste with hot pepper sauce, if desired. *Makes 8 to 10 servings*

Note: For thicker consistency, mash beans slightly with potato masher.

Country Six-Bean Soup

1 jar Country-Six Bean Soup Mix
4 to 5 cups water
1 can (28 ounces) diced tomatoes
   with Italian seasonings

8 ounces smoked sausage links, sliced
   or smoked ham hocks
Hot pepper sauce or red wine
   vinegar (optional)

1. Remove seasoning packet and bay leaves; set aside.

2. Place beans in large bowl; cover with water. Soak 6 to 8 hours or overnight. (To quick soak beans, place beans in large saucepan; cover with water. Bring to a boil over high heat. Boil 2 minutes. Remove from heat; let soak, covered, 1 hour.) Drain beans; discard water.

3. Combine soaked beans, water, tomatoes, sausage, contents of seasoning packet and reserved bay leaves into Dutch oven. Bring to a boil over high heat. Cover; reduce heat and simmer 1½ to 2 hours or until beans are tender. Season to taste with hot pepper sauce, if desired. *Makes 8 to 10 servings*

Note: For thicker consistency, mash beans slightly with potato masher.

Country Six-Bean Soup

1 jar Country-Six Bean Soup Mix
4 to 5 cups water
1 can (28 ounces) diced tomatoes
   with Italian seasonings

8 ounces smoked sausage links, sliced
   or smoked ham hocks
Hot pepper sauce or red wine
   vinegar (optional)

1. Remove seasoning packet and bay leaves; set aside.

2. Place beans in large bowl; cover with water. Soak 6 to 8 hours or overnight. (To quick soak beans, place beans in large saucepan; cover with water. Bring to a boil over high heat. Boil 2 minutes. Remove from heat; let soak, covered, 1 hour.) Drain beans; discard water.

3. Combine soaked beans, water, tomatoes, sausage, contents of seasoning packet and reserved bay leaves into Dutch oven. Bring to a boil over high heat. Cover; reduce heat and simmer 1½ to 2 hours or until beans are tender. Season to taste with hot pepper sauce, if desired. *Makes 8 to 10 servings*

Note: For thicker consistency, mash beans slightly with potato masher.

Country Six-Bean Soup

1 jar Country-Six Bean Soup Mix
4 to 5 cups water
1 can (28 ounces) diced tomatoes
   with Italian seasonings

8 ounces smoked sausage links, sliced
   or smoked ham hocks
Hot pepper sauce or red wine
   vinegar (optional)

1. Remove seasoning packet and bay leaves; set aside.

2. Place beans in large bowl; cover with water. Soak 6 to 8 hours or overnight. (To quick soak beans, place beans in large saucepan; cover with water. Bring to a boil over high heat. Boil 2 minutes. Remove from heat; let soak, covered, 1 hour.) Drain beans; discard water.

3. Combine soaked beans, water, tomatoes, sausage, contents of seasoning packet and reserved bay leaves into Dutch oven. Bring to a boil over high heat. Cover; reduce heat and simmer 1½ to 2 hours or until beans are tender. Season to taste with hot pepper sauce, if desired. *Makes 8 to 10 servings*

Note: For thicker consistency, mash beans slightly with potato masher.

Alphabet Soup in Minutes Mix

1¼ cups uncooked alphabet pasta
2 tablespoons dried vegetable flakes
1 teaspoon chicken bouillon granules
⅛ teaspoon black pepper
½ cup small fish-shaped or cheese crackers

1. Layer ¾ cup pasta, vegetable flakes, bouillon granules, pepper and remaining ½ cup pasta in 1-pint food storage jar with tight-fitting lid. Place crackers into small food storage bag. Close with twist tie and cut off top of bag. Place bag on top of pasta. Close jar.

2. Cover top of jar with fabric; attach gift tag with raffia or ribbon.

Makes one 1-pint jar

Gift Idea: Give this soup mix to your favorite kid along with an alphabet book.

Alphabet Soup in Minutes

1 jar Alphabet Soup in Minutes Mix
4 cups water
¼ cup pasta sauce

1. Remove crackers from jar; set aside.

2. Place water, pasta sauce and remaining contents of jar into large saucepan. Bring to a boil over high heat; reduce heat and simmer 10 minutes, uncovered, or until alphabets are tender. Serve with crackers. *Makes 4 to 5 servings*

Alphabet Soup in Minutes

1 jar Alphabet Soup in Minutes Mix
4 cups water
¼ cup pasta sauce

1. Remove crackers from jar; set aside.

2. Place water, pasta sauce and remaining contents of jar into large saucepan. Bring to a boil over high heat; reduce heat and simmer 10 minutes, uncovered, or until alphabets are tender. Serve with crackers. *Makes 4 to 5 servings*

Alphabet Soup in Minutes

1 jar Alphabet Soup in Minutes Mix
4 cups water
¼ cup pasta sauce

1. Remove crackers from jar; set aside.

2. Place water, pasta sauce and remaining contents of jar into large saucepan. Bring to a boil over high heat; reduce heat and simmer 10 minutes, uncovered, or until alphabets are tender. Serve with crackers. *Makes 4 to 5 servings*

Alphabet Soup in Minutes

1 jar Alphabet Soup in Minutes Mix
4 cups water
¼ cup pasta sauce

1. Remove crackers from jar; set aside.

2. Place water, pasta sauce and remaining contents of jar into large saucepan. Bring to a boil over high heat; reduce heat and simmer 10 minutes, uncovered, or until alphabets are tender. Serve with crackers. *Makes 4 to 5 servings*

Alphabet Soup in Minutes

1 jar Alphabet Soup in Minutes Mix
4 cups water
¼ cup pasta sauce

1. Remove crackers from jar; set aside.

2. Place water, pasta sauce and remaining contents of jar into large saucepan. Bring to a boil over high heat; reduce heat and simmer 10 minutes, uncovered, or until alphabets are tender. Serve with crackers. *Makes 4 to 5 servings*

Alphabet Soup in Minutes

1 jar Alphabet Soup in Minutes Mix
4 cups water
¼ cup pasta sauce

1. Remove crackers from jar; set aside.

2. Place water, pasta sauce and remaining contents of jar into large saucepan. Bring to a boil over high heat; reduce heat and simmer 10 minutes, uncovered, or until alphabets are tender. Serve with crackers. *Makes 4 to 5 servings*

Alphabet Soup in Minutes

1 jar Alphabet Soup in Minutes Mix
4 cups water
¼ cup pasta sauce

1. Remove crackers from jar; set aside.

2. Place water, pasta sauce and remaining contents of jar into large saucepan. Bring to a boil over high heat; reduce heat and simmer 10 minutes, uncovered, or until alphabets are tender. Serve with crackers. *Makes 4 to 5 servings*

Italian-Style Bean Soup Mix

1½ cups dried Great Northern or navy beans
1 tablespoon dried minced onion
2 teaspoons dried basil leaves
2 chicken bouillon cubes, unwrapped
1 teaspoon dried parsley flakes
½ teaspoon dried minced garlic
½ teaspoon black pepper
¼ cup grated Parmesan cheese
1½ cups uncooked medium shell pasta

1. Place Great Northern beans in 1-quart food storage jar with tight-fitting lid. Combine onion, basil, bouillon cubes, parsley, garlic and pepper in small food storage bag. Close bag. Place cheese in small food storage bag. Close bag. Place seasoning and cheese packets in jar spreading out bags to cover beans; add pasta shells. Close jar.

2. Cover top of jar with fabric; attach gift tag with raffia or ribbon.

Makes one 1-quart jar

Italian-Style Bean Soup

1 jar Italian-Style Bean Soup Mix
5 to 6 cups water
1 cup pasta sauce
8 ounces baby spinach leaves (optional)
  Salt and pepper

1. Remove pasta, cheese and seasoning packets from jar; set aside. Place beans in large bowl; cover with water. Soak 6 to 8 hours or overnight. (To quick soak beans, place beans in large saucepan; cover with water. Bring to a boil over high heat. Boil 2 minutes. Remove from heat; let soak, covered, 1 hour.) Drain beans; discard water.

2. Combine soaked beans, water, pasta sauce and contents of seasoning packet in Dutch oven. Bring to a boil over high heat. Cover; reduce heat and simmer 2 to 2½ hours or until tender. Add shells and spinach, if desired, to Dutch oven. Cover and simmer 15 to 20 minutes or until pasta is tender. Season to taste. Serve with Parmesan cheese. *Makes 8 to 10 servings*

Variation: Add 8 slices crisp-cooked bacon, crumbled.

Italian-Style Bean Soup

1 jar Italian-Style Bean Soup Mix
5 to 6 cups water
1 cup pasta sauce

8 ounces baby spinach leaves
(optional)
Salt and pepper

1. Remove pasta, cheese and seasoning packets from jar; set aside. Place beans in large bowl; cover with water. Soak 6 to 8 hours or overnight. (To quick soak beans, place beans in large saucepan; cover with water. Bring to a boil over high heat. Boil 2 minutes. Remove from heat; let soak, covered, 1 hour.) Drain beans; discard water.

2. Combine soaked beans, water, pasta sauce and contents of seasoning packet in Dutch oven. Bring to a boil over high heat. Cover; reduce heat and simmer 2 to 2½ hours or until tender. Add shells and spinach, if desired, to Dutch oven. Cover and simmer 15 to 20 minutes or until pasta is tender. Season to taste. Serve with Parmesan cheese.

Makes 8 to 10 servings

Variation: Add 8 slices crisp-cooked bacon, crumbled.

Italian-Style Bean Soup

1 jar Italian-Style Bean Soup Mix
5 to 6 cups water
1 cup pasta sauce

8 ounces baby spinach leaves
(optional)
Salt and pepper

1. Remove pasta, cheese and seasoning packets from jar; set aside. Place beans in large bowl; cover with water. Soak 6 to 8 hours or overnight. (To quick soak beans, place beans in large saucepan; cover with water. Bring to a boil over high heat. Boil 2 minutes. Remove from heat; let soak, covered, 1 hour.) Drain beans; discard water.

2. Combine soaked beans, water, pasta sauce and contents of seasoning packet in Dutch oven. Bring to a boil over high heat. Cover; reduce heat and simmer 2 to 2½ hours or until tender. Add shells and spinach, if desired, to Dutch oven. Cover and simmer 15 to 20 minutes or until pasta is tender. Season to taste. Serve with Parmesan cheese.

Makes 8 to 10 servings

Variation: Add 8 slices crisp-cooked bacon, crumbled.

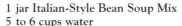

Italian-Style Bean Soup

1 jar Italian-Style Bean Soup Mix
5 to 6 cups water
1 cup pasta sauce

8 ounces baby spinach leaves
(optional)
Salt and pepper

1. Remove pasta, cheese and seasoning packets from jar; set aside. Place beans in large bowl; cover with water. Soak 6 to 8 hours or overnight. (To quick soak beans, place beans in large saucepan; cover with water. Bring to a boil over high heat. Boil 2 minutes. Remove from heat; let soak, covered, 1 hour.) Drain beans; discard water.

2. Combine soaked beans, water, pasta sauce and contents of seasoning packet in Dutch oven. Bring to a boil over high heat. Cover; reduce heat and simmer 2 to 2½ hours or until tender. Add shells and spinach, if desired, to Dutch oven. Cover and simmer 15 to 20 minutes or until pasta is tender. Season to taste. Serve with Parmesan cheese.

Makes 8 to 10 servings

Variation: Add 8 slices crisp-cooked bacon, crumbled.

Italial-Style Bean Soup

1 jar Italian-Style Bean Soup Mix
5 to 6 cups water
1 cup pasta sauce

8 ounces baby spinach leaves
(optional)
Salt and pepper

1. Remove pasta, cheese and seasoning packets from jar; set aside. Place beans in large bowl; cover with water. Soak 6 to 8 hours or overnight. (To quick soak beans, place beans in large saucepan; cover with water. Bring to a boil over high heat. Boil 2 minutes. Remove from heat; let soak, covered, 1 hour.) Drain beans; discard water.

2. Combine soaked beans, water, pasta sauce and contents of seasoning packet in Dutch oven. Bring to a boil over high heat. Cover; reduce heat and simmer 2 to 2½ hours or until tender. Add shells and spinach, if desired, to Dutch oven. Cover and simmer 15 to 20 minutes or until pasta is tender. Season to taste. Serve with Parmesan cheese.

Makes 8 to 10 servings

Variation: Add 8 slices crisp-cooked bacon, crumbled.

Italian-Style Bean Soup

1 jar Italian-Style Bean Soup Mix
5 to 6 cups water
1 cup pasta sauce

8 ounces baby spinach leaves
(optional)
Salt and pepper

1. Remove pasta, cheese and seasoning packets from jar; set aside. Place beans in large bowl; cover with water. Soak 6 to 8 hours or overnight. (To quick soak beans, place beans in large saucepan; cover with water. Bring to a boil over high heat. Boil 2 minutes. Remove from heat; let soak, covered, 1 hour.) Drain beans; discard water.

2. Combine soaked beans, water, pasta sauce and contents of seasoning packet in Dutch oven. Bring to a boil over high heat. Cover; reduce heat and simmer 2 to 2½ hours or until tender. Add shells and spinach, if desired, to Dutch oven. Cover and simmer 15 to 20 minutes or until pasta is tender. Season to taste. Serve with Parmesan cheese.

Makes 8 to 10 servings

Variation: Add 8 slices crisp-cooked bacon, crumbled.

Italian-Style Bean Soup

1 jar Italian-Style Bean Soup Mix
5 to 6 cups water
1 cup pasta sauce

8 ounces baby spinach leaves
(optional)
Salt and pepper

1. Remove pasta, cheese and seasoning packets from jar; set aside. Place beans in large bowl; cover with water. Soak 6 to 8 hours or overnight. (To quick soak beans, place beans in large saucepan; cover with water. Bring to a boil over high heat. Boil 2 minutes. Remove from heat; let soak, covered, 1 hour.) Drain beans; discard water.

2. Combine soaked beans, water, pasta sauce and contents of seasoning packet in Dutch oven. Bring to a boil over high heat. Cover; reduce heat and simmer 2 to 2½ hours or until tender. Add shells and spinach, if desired, to Dutch oven. Cover and simmer 15 to 20 minutes or until pasta is tender. Season to taste. Serve with Parmesan cheese.

Makes 8 to 10 servings

Variation: Add 8 slices crisp-cooked bacon, crumbled.

Green & Yellow Split Pea Soup Mix

¾ cup dried green split peas
¾ cup dried yellow split peas
1 bay leaf
1 package dried vegetable soup and dip mix
1 teaspoon chicken bouillon granules
½ teaspoon lemon pepper

1. Layer green and yellow split peas in 1-pint food storage jar with tight-fitting lid. Slide bay leaf down side of jar. Place soup and dip mix, bouillon granules and lemon pepper in small food storage bag. Close with twist tie and cut off top of bag. Place bag on top of peas. Close jar.

2. Cover top of jar with fabric; attach gift tag with raffia or ribbon.

Makes one 1-pint jar

Gift Idea: Assemble a jar of Green & Yellow Split Pea Soup Mix with a package of corn bread mix in a decorated gift basket or bag.

Green & Yellow Split Pea Soup

1 jar Green & Yellow Split Pea Soup Mix
5 to 6 cups water
1 to 2 smoked ham hocks *or* 1 meaty ham bone

1. Remove seasoning packet and bay leaf from jar; set aside.

2. Sort and rinse peas thoroughly. Combine peas, water, ham hock, contents of seasoning packet and bay leaf in slow cooker. Cover and cook on LOW 4 to 5 hours or until peas are tender.

3. Remove and discard bay leaf. Take out ham hock; remove skin and cut meat from bones into pieces. Return meat to pan. Heat through. *Makes 4 to 5 servings*

Conventional Method: Simmer bean mixture in step 2 in Dutch oven, partially covered, 1 hour or until tender. Continue as directed in step 3.

Green & Yellow Split Pea Soup

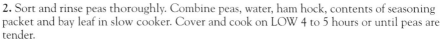

1 jar Green & Yellow Split Pea Soup
   Mix
5 to 6 cups water

1 to 2 smoked ham hocks *or* 1 meaty
   ham bone

1. Remove seasoning packet and bay leaf from jar; set aside.

2. Sort and rinse peas thoroughly. Combine peas, water, ham hock, contents of seasoning packet and bay leaf in slow cooker. Cover and cook on LOW 4 to 5 hours or until peas are tender.

3. Remove and discard bay leaf. Take out ham hock; remove skin and cut meat from bone into pieces. Return meat to pan. Heat through.   *Makes 4 to 5 servings*

Conventional Method: Simmer bean mixture in step 2 in Dutch oven, partially covered, 1 hour or until tender. Continue as directed in step 3.

Green & Yellow Split Pea Soup

1 jar Green & Yellow Split Pea Soup
   Mix
5 to 6 cups water

1 to 2 smoked ham hocks *or* 1 meaty
   ham bone

1. Remove seasoning packet and bay leaf from jar; set aside.

2. Sort and rinse peas thoroughly. Combine peas, water, ham hock, contents of seasoning packet and bay leaf in slow cooker. Cover and cook on LOW 4 to 5 hours or until peas are tender.

3. Remove and discard bay leaf. Take out ham hock; remove skin and cut meat from bone into pieces. Return meat to pan. Heat through.   *Makes 4 to 5 servings*

Conventional Method: Simmer bean mixture in step 2 in Dutch oven, partially covered, 1 hour or until tender. Continue as directed in step 3.

Green & Yellow Split Pea Soup

1 jar Green & Yellow Split Pea Soup
   Mix
5 to 6 cups water

1 to 2 smoked ham hocks *or* 1 meaty
   ham bone

1. Remove seasoning packet and bay leaf from jar; set aside.

2. Sort and rinse peas thoroughly. Combine peas, water, ham hock, contents of seasoning packet and bay leaf in slow cooker. Cover and cook on LOW 4 to 5 hours or until peas are tender.

3. Remove and discard bay leaf. Take out ham hock; remove skin and cut meat from bone into pieces. Return meat to pan. Heat through.   *Makes 4 to 5 servings*

Conventional Method: Simmer bean mixture in step 2 in Dutch oven, partially covered, 1 hour or until tender. Continue as directed in step 3.

Green & Yellow Split Pea Soup

1 jar Green & Yellow Split Pea Soup
    Mix
5 to 6 cups water

1 to 2 smoked ham hocks *or* 1 meaty
    ham bone

1. Remove seasoning packet and bay leaf from jar; set aside.

2. Sort and rinse peas thoroughly. Combine peas, water, ham hock, contents of seasoning packet and bay leaf in slow cooker. Cover and cook on LOW 4 to 5 hours or until peas are tender.

3. Remove and discard bay leaf. Take out ham hock; remove skin and cut meat from bone into pieces. Return meat to pan. Heat through.   *Makes 4 to 5 servings*

Conventional Method: Simmer bean mixture in step 2 in Dutch oven, partially covered, 1 hour or until tender. Continue as directed in step 3.

Green & Yellow Split Pea Soup

1 jar Green & Yellow Split Pea Soup
    Mix
5 to 6 cups water

1 to 2 smoked ham hocks *or* 1 meaty
    ham bone

1. Remove seasoning packet and bay leaf from jar; set aside.

2. Sort and rinse peas thoroughly. Combine peas, water, ham hock, contents of seasoning packet and bay leaf in slow cooker. Cover and cook on LOW 4 to 5 hours or until peas are tender.

3. Remove and discard bay leaf. Take out ham hock; remove skin and cut meat from bone into pieces. Return meat to pan. Heat through.   *Makes 4 to 5 servings*

Conventional Method: Simmer bean mixture in step 2 in Dutch oven, partially covered, 1 hour or until tender. Continue as directed in step 3.

Green & Yellow Split Pea Soup

1 jar Green & Yellow Split Pea Soup
    Mix
5 to 6 cups water

1 to 2 smoked ham hocks *or* 1 meaty
    ham bone

1. Remove seasoning packet and bay leaf from jar; set aside.

2. Sort and rinse peas thoroughly. Combine peas, water, ham hock, contents of seasoning packet and bay leaf in slow cooker. Cover and cook on LOW 4 to 5 hours or until peas are tender.

3. Remove and discard bay leaf. Take out ham hock; remove skin and cut meat from bone into pieces. Return meat to pan. Heat through.   *Makes 4 to 5 servings*

Conventional Method: Simmer bean mixture in step 2 in Dutch oven, partially covered, 1 hour or until tender. Continue as directed in step 3.

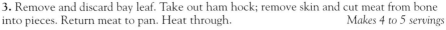

Southwestern Bean Chili & Rice Mix

½ cup dried red kidney beans
½ cup dried chick-peas or navy beans
½ cup dried black beans
1 bay leaf
2 tablespoons dried minced onion
1 tablespoon chicken bouillon granules
2 teaspoons minced garlic
2 teaspoons chili powder
1 teaspoon cocoa powder
1 teaspoon ground cumin
1 teaspoon dried oregano leaves
¼ teaspoon ground red pepper
2 bags boil-in-bag rice

1. Place kidney beans, chick-peas and black beans in 1-quart food storage jar with tight-fitting lid. Slide bay leaf down side of jar. Combine onion, bouillon granules, garlic, chili powder, cocoa, cumin, oregano and red pepper in small food storage bag. Close with twist tie and cut off top of bag. Place on top of beans. Add bags of rice. Close jar.

2. Cover top of jar with fabric; attach gift tag with raffia or ribbon.

Makes one 1-quart jar

Southwestern Bean Chili & Rice

1 jar Southwestern Bean Chili & Rice Mix
3 to 4 cups water
2 cans (14½ ounces) diced tomatoes with green chilies,
    undrained
1 can (8 ounces) tomato sauce
    Shredded cheese

1. Remove rice and seasoning packet from jar; set aside. Place beans in large bowl; cover with water. Soak 6 to 8 hours or overnight. (To quick soak beans, place beans in large saucepan; cover with water. Bring to a boil over high heat. Boil 2 minutes. Remove from heat; let soak, covered, 1 hour.) Drain beans; discard water.

2. Combine soaked beans, water, tomatoes, tomato sauce and contents of seasoning packet in Dutch oven. Bring to a boil over high heat. Cover; reduce heat and simmer 1½ to 2 hours or until beans are tender. Submerge bags of rice in boiling salted water. Cook 10 minutes. Drain rice. Serve with chili and cheese.

Makes 6 to 8 servings

Southwestern Bean Chili & Rice

1 jar Southwestern Bean Chili & Rice
 Mix
3 to 4 cups water
2 cans (14½ ounces) diced tomatoes
 with green chilies, undrained

1 can (8 ounces) tomato sauce
Shredded cheese

1. Remove rice and seasoning packet from jar; set aside. Place beans in large bowl; cover with water. Soak 6 to 8 hours or overnight. (To quick soak beans, place beans in large saucepan; cover with water. Bring to a boil over high heat. Boil 2 minutes. Remove from heat; let soak, covered, 1 hour.) Drain beans; discard water.

2. Combine soaked beans, water, tomatoes, tomato sauce and contents of seasoning packet in Dutch oven. Bring to a boil over high heat. Cover; reduce heat and simmer 1½ to 2 hours or until beans are tender. Submerge bags of rice in boiling salted water. Cook 10 minutes. Drain rice. Serve with chili and cheese.   *Makes 6 to 8 servings*

Southwestern Bean Chili & Rice

1 jar Southwestern Bean Chili & Rice
 Mix
3 to 4 cups water
2 cans (14½ ounces) diced tomatoes
 with green chilies, undrained

1 can (8 ounces) tomato sauce
Shredded cheese

1. Remove rice and seasoning packet from jar; set aside. Place beans in large bowl; cover with water. Soak 6 to 8 hours or overnight. (To quick soak beans, place beans in large saucepan; cover with water. Bring to a boil over high heat. Boil 2 minutes. Remove from heat; let soak, covered, 1 hour.) Drain beans; discard water.

2. Combine soaked beans, water, tomatoes, tomato sauce and contents of seasoning packet in Dutch oven. Bring to a boil over high heat. Cover; reduce heat and simmer 1½ to 2 hours or until beans are tender. Submerge bags of rice in boiling salted water. Cook 10 minutes. Drain rice. Serve with chili and cheese.   *Makes 6 to 8 servings*

Southwestern Bean Chili & Rice

1 jar Southwestern Bean Chili & Rice
 Mix
3 to 4 cups water
2 cans (14½ ounces) diced tomatoes
 with green chilies, undrained

1 can (8 ounces) tomato sauce
Shredded cheese

1. Remove rice and seasoning packet from jar; set aside. Place beans in large bowl; cover with water. Soak 6 to 8 hours or overnight. (To quick soak beans, place beans in large saucepan; cover with water. Bring to a boil over high heat. Boil 2 minutes. Remove from heat; let soak, covered, 1 hour.) Drain beans; discard water.

2. Combine soaked beans, water, tomatoes, tomato sauce and contents of seasoning packet in Dutch oven. Bring to a boil over high heat. Cover; reduce heat and simmer 1½ to 2 hours or until beans are tender. Submerge bags of rice in boiling salted water. Cook 10 minutes. Drain rice. Serve with chili and cheese.   *Makes 6 to 8 servings*

Southwestern Bean Chili & Rice

1 jar Southwestern Bean Chili & Rice
   Mix
3 to 4 cups water
2 cans (14½ ounces) diced tomatoes
   with green chilies, undrained

1 can (8 ounces) tomato sauce
Shredded cheese

1. Remove rice and seasoning packet from jar; set aside. Place beans in large bowl; cover with water. Soak 6 to 8 hours or overnight. (To quick soak beans, place beans in large saucepan; cover with water. Bring to a boil over high heat. Boil 2 minutes. Remove from heat; let soak, covered, 1 hour.) Drain beans; discard water.

2. Combine soaked beans, water, tomatoes, tomato sauce and contents of seasoning packet in Dutch oven. Bring to a boil over high heat. Cover; reduce heat and simmer 1½ to 2 hours or until beans are tender. Submerge bags of rice in boiling salted water. Cook 10 minutes. Drain rice. Serve with chili and cheese. *Makes 6 to 8 servings*

Southwestern Bean Chili & Rice

1 jar Southwestern Bean Chili & Rice
   Mix
3 to 4 cups water
2 cans (14½ ounces) diced tomatoes
   with green chilies, undrained

1 can (8 ounces) tomato sauce
Shredded cheese

1. Remove rice and seasoning packet from jar; set aside. Place beans in large bowl; cover with water. Soak 6 to 8 hours or overnight. (To quick soak beans, place beans in large saucepan; cover with water. Bring to a boil over high heat. Boil 2 minutes. Remove from heat; let soak, covered, 1 hour.) Drain beans; discard water.

2. Combine soaked beans, water, tomatoes, tomato sauce and contents of seasoning packet in Dutch oven. Bring to a boil over high heat. Cover; reduce heat and simmer 1½ to 2 hours or until beans are tender. Submerge bags of rice in boiling salted water. Cook 10 minutes. Drain rice. Serve with chili and cheese. *Makes 6 to 8 servings*

Southwestern Bean Chili & Rice

1 jar Southwestern Bean Chili & Rice
   Mix
3 to 4 cups water
2 cans (14½ ounces) diced tomatoes
   with green chilies, undrained

1 can (8 ounces) tomato sauce
Shredded cheese

1. Remove rice and seasoning packet from jar; set aside. Place beans in large bowl; cover with water. Soak 6 to 8 hours or overnight. (To quick soak beans, place beans in large saucepan; cover with water. Bring to a boil over high heat. Boil 2 minutes. Remove from heat; let soak, covered, 1 hour.) Drain beans; discard water.

2. Combine soaked beans, water, tomatoes, tomato sauce and contents of seasoning packet in Dutch oven. Bring to a boil over high heat. Cover; reduce heat and simmer 1½ to 2 hours or until beans are tender. Submerge bags of rice in boiling salted water. Cook 10 minutes. Drain rice. Serve with chili and cheese. *Makes 6 to 8 servings*

Spicy Chili Mac Mix

¾ cup dried pinto beans
¾ cup dried red kidney beans
1 package (about 1¼ ounces) chili seasoning mix
2 tablespoons dried minced onion
2 teaspoons beef bouillon granules
¼ teaspoon red pepper flakes
1½ cups uncooked rotini pasta

1. Layer pinto and kidney beans in 1-quart food storage jar with tight-fitting lid. Combine chili seasoning, onion, bouillon granules and pepper flakes in small food storage bag. Close bag with twist tie and place on top of beans spreading out bag to cover beans. Add pasta. Close jar.

2. Cover top of jar with fabric; attach gift tag with raffia or ribbon.

Makes one 1-quart jar

Spicy Chili Mac

1 jar Spicy Chili Mac Mix
4 to 5 cups water
2 cans (14½ ounces) tomatoes with green chilies, undrained
1 pound ground beef or ground turkey, browned and drained
   Shredded Cheddar cheese (optional)

1. Remove pasta and seasoning packet from jar; set aside.

2. Place beans in large bowl; cover with water. Soak 6 to 8 hours or overnight. (To quick soak beans, place beans in large saucepan; cover with water. Bring to a boil over high heat. Boil 2 minutes. Remove from heat; let soak, covered, 1 hour.) Drain beans; discard water.

3. Combine soaked beans, water, tomatoes, ground beef and contents of seasoning packet in Dutch oven. Bring to a boil over high heat. Cover; reduce heat and simmer 1½ hours. Add pasta and simmer 30 to 45 minutes. Serve with Cheddar cheese, if desired.

Makes 8 to 10 servings

Spicy Chili Mac

1 jar Spicy Chili Mac Mix
4 to 5 cups water
2 cans (14½ ounces) tomatoes with
   green chilies, undrained

1 pound ground beef or ground
   turkey, browned and drained
Shredded Cheddar cheese (optional)

1. Remove pasta and seasoning packet from jar; set aside.

2. Place beans in large bowl; cover with water. Soak 6 to 8 hours or overnight. (To quick soak beans, place beans in large saucepan; cover with water. Bring to a boil over high heat. Boil 2 minutes. Remove from heat; let soak, covered, 1 hour.) Drain beans; discard water.

3. Combine soaked beans, water, tomatoes, ground beef and contents of seasoning packet in Dutch oven. Bring to a boil over high heat. Cover; reduce heat and simmer 1½ hours. Add pasta and simmer 30 to 45 minutes. Serve with Cheddar cheese, if desired.

Makes 8 to 10 servings

Spicy Chili Mac

1 jar Spicy Chili Mac Mix
4 to 5 cups water
2 cans (14½ ounces) tomatoes with
   green chilies, undrained

1 pound ground beef or ground
   turkey, browned and drained
Shredded Cheddar cheese (optional)

1. Remove pasta and seasoning packet from jar; set aside.

2. Place beans in large bowl; cover with water. Soak 6 to 8 hours or overnight. (To quick soak beans, place beans in large saucepan; cover with water. Bring to a boil over high heat. Boil 2 minutes. Remove from heat; let soak, covered, 1 hour.) Drain beans; discard water.

3. Combine soaked beans, water, tomatoes, ground beef and contents of seasoning packet in Dutch oven. Bring to a boil over high heat. Cover; reduce heat and simmer 1½ hours. Add pasta and simmer 30 to 45 minutes. Serve with Cheddar cheese, if desired.

Makes 8 to 10 servings

Spicy Chili Mac

1 jar Spicy Chili Mac Mix
4 to 5 cups water
2 cans (14½ ounces) tomatoes with
   green chilies, undrained

1 pound ground beef or ground
   turkey, browned and drained
Shredded Cheddar cheese (optional)

1. Remove pasta and seasoning packet from jar; set aside.

2. Place beans in large bowl; cover with water. Soak 6 to 8 hours or overnight. (To quick soak beans, place beans in large saucepan; cover with water. Bring to a boil over high heat. Boil 2 minutes. Remove from heat; let soak, covered, 1 hour.) Drain beans; discard water.

3. Combine soaked beans, water, tomatoes, ground beef and contents of seasoning packet in Dutch oven. Bring to a boil over high heat. Cover; reduce heat and simmer 1½ hours. Add pasta and simmer 30 to 45 minutes. Serve with Cheddar cheese, if desired.

Makes 8 to 10 servings

Spicy Chili Mac

1 jar Spicy Chili Mac Mix
4 to 5 cups water
2 cans (14½ ounces) tomatoes with
green chilies, undrained

1 pound ground beef or ground
turkey, browned and drained
Shredded Cheddar cheese (optional)

1. Remove pasta and seasoning packet from jar; set aside.

2. Place beans in large bowl; cover with water. Soak 6 to 8 hours or overnight. (To quick soak beans, place beans in large saucepan; cover with water. Bring to a boil over high heat. Boil 2 minutes. Remove from heat; let soak, covered, 1 hour.) Drain beans; discard water.

3. Combine soaked beans, water, tomatoes, ground beef and contents of seasoning packet in Dutch oven. Bring to a boil over high heat. Cover; reduce heat and simmer 1½ hours. Add pasta and simmer 30 to 45 minutes. Serve with Cheddar cheese, if desired.

Makes 8 to 10 servings

Spicy Chili Mac

1 jar Spicy Chili Mac Mix
4 to 5 cups water
2 cans (14½ ounces) tomatoes with
green chilies, undrained

1 pound ground beef or ground
turkey, browned and drained
Shredded Cheddar cheese (optional)

1. Remove pasta and seasoning packet from jar; set aside.

2. Place beans in large bowl; cover with water. Soak 6 to 8 hours or overnight. (To quick soak beans, place beans in large saucepan; cover with water. Bring to a boil over high heat. Boil 2 minutes. Remove from heat; let soak, covered, 1 hour.) Drain beans; discard water.

3. Combine soaked beans, water, tomatoes, ground beef and contents of seasoning packet in Dutch oven. Bring to a boil over high heat. Cover; reduce heat and simmer 1½ hours. Add pasta and simmer 30 to 45 minutes. Serve with Cheddar cheese, if desired.

Makes 8 to 10 servings

Spicy Chili Mac

1 jar Spicy Chili Mac Mix
4 to 5 cups water
2 cans (14½ ounces) tomatoes with
green chilies, undrained

1 pound ground beef or ground
turkey, browned and drained
Shredded Cheddar cheese (optional)

1. Remove pasta and seasoning packet from jar; set aside.

2. Place beans in large bowl; cover with water. Soak 6 to 8 hours or overnight. (To quick soak beans, place beans in large saucepan; cover with water. Bring to a boil over high heat. Boil 2 minutes. Remove from heat; let soak, covered, 1 hour.) Drain beans; discard water.

3. Combine soaked beans, water, tomatoes, ground beef and contents of seasoning packet in Dutch oven. Bring to a boil over high heat. Cover; reduce heat and simmer 1½ hours. Add pasta and simmer 30 to 45 minutes. Serve with Cheddar cheese, if desired.

Makes 8 to 10 servings

Taco Bean Chili Mix

½ cup dried kidney beans
½ cup dried pinto beans
½ cup dried red beans
1 package (1¼ ounces) taco seasoning mix
1 tablespoon dried minced onion
½ teaspoon chili powder or chipotle chili pepper seasoning
¼ teaspoon ground cumin
1½ cups tortilla chips

1. Layer kidney beans, pinto beans and red beans in 1-quart jar with tight-fitting lid. Place taco seasoning mix, onion, chili powder and cumin in small food storage bag. Close with twist tie. Place in jar spreading out to cover beans. Add tortilla chips. Close jar.

2. Cover top of jar with fabric; attach gift tag with raffia or ribbon.

Makes one 1-quart jar

Taco Bean Chili

1 jar Taco Bean Chili Mix
4 cups water
1 can (14½ ounces) diced tomatoes with green chilies,
    undrained
1 can (8 ounces) tomato sauce
1 pound ground beef or ground turkey, browned and drained
    Shredded cheese, chopped lettuce, sliced black olives
    (optional)

1. Remove chips and seasoning packet from jar; set aside. Place beans in large bowl; cover with water. Soak 6 to 8 hours or overnight. (To quick soak beans, place beans in large saucepan; cover with water. Bring to a boil over high heat. Boil 2 minutes. Remove from heat; let soak, covered, 1 hour.) Drain beans; discard water.

2. Place soaked beans, water, tomatoes, tomato sauce, ground beef and contents of seasoning packet in Dutch oven. Bring to a boil over high heat. Cover; reduce heat and simmer 1½ to 2 hours or until beans are tender. Crush tortilla chips. Stir into chili and cook 5 to 10 minutes to thicken. Serve with accompaniments.

Makes 6 to 8 servings

Taco Bean Chili

1 jar Taco Bean Chili Mix
4 cups water
1 can (14½ ounces) diced tomatoes
   with green chilies, undrained
1 can (8 ounces) tomato sauce

1 pound ground beef or ground
   turkey, browned and drained
Shredded cheese, chopped lettuce,
   sliced black olives (optional)

1. Remove chips and seasoning packet from jar; set aside. Place beans in large bowl; cover with water. Soak 6 to 8 hours or overnight. (To quick soak beans, place beans in large saucepan; cover with water. Bring to a boil over high heat. Boil 2 minutes. Remove from heat; let soak, covered, 1 hour.) Drain beans; discard water.

2. Place soaked beans, water, tomatoes, tomato sauce, ground beef and contents of seasoning packet in Dutch oven. Bring to a boil over high heat. Cover; reduce heat and simmer 1½ to 2 hours or until beans are tender. Crush tortilla chips. Stir into chili and cook 5 to 10 minutes to thicken. Serve with accompaniments. *Makes 6 to 8 servings*

Taco Bean Chili

1 jar Taco Bean Chili Mix
4 cups water
1 can (14½ ounces) diced tomatoes
   with green chilies, undrained
1 can (8 ounces) tomato sauce

1 pound ground beef or ground
   turkey, browned and drained
Shredded cheese, chopped lettuce,
   sliced black olives (optional)

1. Remove chips and seasoning packet from jar; set aside. Place beans in large bowl; cover with water. Soak 6 to 8 hours or overnight. (To quick soak beans, place beans in large saucepan; cover with water. Bring to a boil over high heat. Boil 2 minutes. Remove from heat; let soak, covered, 1 hour.) Drain beans; discard water.

2. Place soaked beans, water, tomatoes, tomato sauce, ground beef and contents of seasoning packet in Dutch oven. Bring to a boil over high heat. Cover; reduce heat and simmer 1½ to 2 hours or until beans are tender. Crush tortilla chips. Stir into chili and cook 5 to 10 minutes to thicken. Serve with accompaniments. *Makes 6 to 8 servings*

Taco Bean Chili

1 jar Taco Bean Chili Mix
4 cups water
1 can (14½ ounces) diced tomatoes
   with green chilies, undrained
1 can (8 ounces) tomato sauce

1 pound ground beef or ground
   turkey, browned and drained
Shredded cheese, chopped lettuce,
   sliced black olives (optional)

1. Remove chips and seasoning packet from jar; set aside. Place beans in large bowl; cover with water. Soak 6 to 8 hours or overnight. (To quick soak beans, place beans in large saucepan; cover with water. Bring to a boil over high heat. Boil 2 minutes. Remove from heat; let soak, covered, 1 hour.) Drain beans; discard water.

2. Place soaked beans, water, tomatoes, tomato sauce, ground beef and contents of seasoning packet in Dutch oven. Bring to a boil over high heat. Cover; reduce heat and simmer 1½ to 2 hours or until beans are tender. Crush tortilla chips. Stir into chili and cook 5 to 10 minutes to thicken. Serve with accompaniments. *Makes 6 to 8 servings*

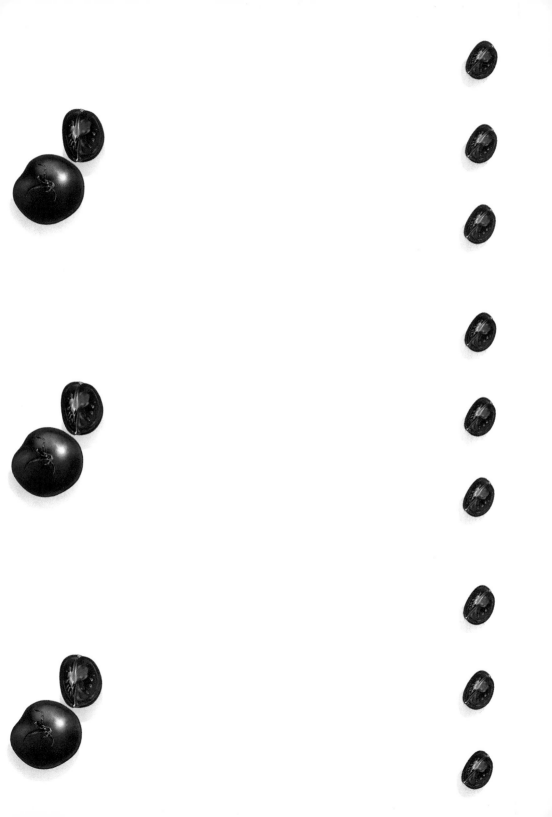

Taco Bean Chili

1 jar Taco Bean Chili Mix
4 cups water
1 can (14½ ounces) diced tomatoes
   with green chilies, undrained
1 can (8 ounces) tomato sauce

1 pound ground beef or ground
   turkey, browned and drained
Shredded cheese, chopped lettuce,
   sliced black olives (optional)

1. Remove chips and seasoning packet from jar; set aside. Place beans in large bowl; cover with water. Soak 6 to 8 hours or overnight. (To quick soak beans, place beans in large saucepan; cover with water. Bring to a boil over high heat. Boil 2 minutes. Remove from heat; let soak, covered, 1 hour.) Drain beans; discard water.

2. Place soaked beans, water, tomatoes, tomato sauce, ground beef and contents of seasoning packet in Dutch oven. Bring to a boil over high heat. Cover; reduce heat and simmer 1½ to 2 hours or until beans are tender. Crush tortilla chips. Stir into chili and cook 5 to 10 minutes to thicken. Serve with accompaniments. *Makes 6 to 8 servings*

Taco Bean Chili

1 jar Taco Bean Chili Mix
4 cups water
1 can (14½ ounces) diced tomatoes
   with green chilies, undrained
1 can (8 ounces) tomato sauce

1 pound ground beef or ground
   turkey, browned and drained
Shredded cheese, chopped lettuce,
   sliced black olives (optional)

1. Remove chips and seasoning packet from jar; set aside. Place beans in large bowl; cover with water. Soak 6 to 8 hours or overnight. (To quick soak beans, place beans in large saucepan; cover with water. Bring to a boil over high heat. Boil 2 minutes. Remove from heat; let soak, covered, 1 hour.) Drain beans; discard water.

2. Place soaked beans, water, tomatoes, tomato sauce, ground beef and contents of seasoning packet in Dutch oven. Bring to a boil over high heat. Cover; reduce heat and simmer 1½ to 2 hours or until beans are tender. Crush tortilla chips. Stir into chili and cook 5 to 10 minutes to thicken. Serve with accompaniments. *Makes 6 to 8 servings*

Taco Bean Chili

1 jar Taco Bean Chili Mix
4 cups water
1 can (14½ ounces) diced tomatoes
   with green chilies, undrained
1 can (8 ounces) tomato sauce

1 pound ground beef or ground
   turkey, browned and drained
Shredded cheese, chopped lettuce,
   sliced black olives (optional)

1. Remove chips and seasoning packet from jar; set aside. Place beans in large bowl; cover with water. Soak 6 to 8 hours or overnight. (To quick soak beans, place beans in large saucepan; cover with water. Bring to a boil over high heat. Boil 2 minutes. Remove from heat; let soak, covered, 1 hour.) Drain beans; discard water.

2. Place soaked beans, water, tomatoes, tomato sauce, ground beef and contents of seasoning packet in Dutch oven. Bring to a boil over high heat. Cover; reduce heat and simmer 1½ to 2 hours or until beans are tender. Crush tortilla chips. Stir into chili and cook 5 to 10 minutes to thicken. Serve with accompaniments. *Makes 6 to 8 servings*

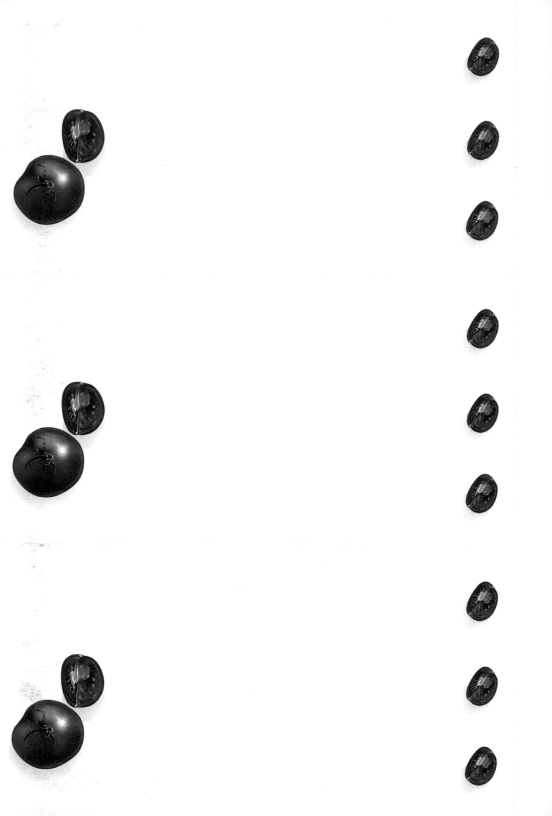

Chili Barbecue Beans Mix

1 cup dried Great Northern beans
1 cup dried red beans or dried kidney beans
1 cup dried baby lima beans
2 bay leaves
¼ cup brown sugar
2 tablespoons dried minced onion
2 beef bouillon cubes, unwrapped
1 teaspoon dried mustard
1 teaspoon chili powder
1 teaspoon dried minced garlic
½ teaspoon black pepper
¼ teaspoon red pepper flakes

1. Layer Great Northern beans, red beans and lima beans in 1-quart food storage jar with tight-fitting lid. Slide bay leaves down side of jar. Combine sugar, onion, bouillon cubes, mustard, chili powder, garlic, black pepper and red pepper flakes into small food storage bag. Close bag with twist tie and cut off top of bag. Place on top of beans. Close jar.

2. Cover top of jar with fabric; attach gift tag with raffia or ribbon.

Makes one 1-quart jar

Chili Barbecue Beans

1 jar Chili Barbecue Beans Mix
3 to 4 cups water
8 slices crisp-cooked bacon, crumbled *or* 8 ounces smoked
    sausage, sliced
1 to 1½ cups barbecue sauce

1. Remove seasoning packet and bay leaves from jar; set aside.

2. Place beans in large bowl; cover with water. Soak 6 to 8 hours or overnight. (To quick soak beans, place beans in large saucepan; cover with water. Bring to a boil over high heat. Boil 2 minutes. Remove from heat; let soak, covered, 1 hour.) Drain beans; discard water.

3. Combine soaked beans, water, bacon, contents of seasoning packet and bay leaves in Dutch oven. Bring to a boil over high heat. Cover; reduce heat and simmer 1½ hours. Add barbecue sauce and simmer, uncovered, 1 hour or until beans are tender. Remove and discard bay leaves.   *Makes 8 to 10 servings*

Chili Barbecue Beans

1 jar Chili Barbecue Beans Mix
3 to 4 cups water
8 slices crisp-cooked bacon, crumbled
   or 8 ounces smoked sausage,
   sliced

1 to 1½ cups barbecue sauce

1. Remove seasoning packet and bay leaves from jar; set aside.

2. Place beans in large bowl; cover with water. Soak 6 to 8 hours or overnight. (To quick soak beans, place beans in large saucepan; cover with water. Bring to a boil over high heat. Boil 2 minutes. Remove from heat; let soak, covered, 1 hour.) Drain beans; discard water.

3. Combine soaked beans, water, bacon, contents of seasoning packet and bay leaves in Dutch oven. Bring to a boil over high heat. Cover; reduce heat and simmer 1½ hours. Add barbecue sauce and simmer, uncovered, 1 hour or until beans are tender. Remove and discard bay leaves.

Makes 8 to 10 servings

Chili Barbecue Beans

1 jar Chili Barbecue Beans Mix
3 to 4 cups water
8 slices crisp-cooked bacon, crumbled
   or 8 ounces smoked sausage,
   sliced

1 to 1½ cups barbecue sauce

1. Remove seasoning packet and bay leaves from jar; set aside.

2. Place beans in large bowl; cover with water. Soak 6 to 8 hours or overnight. (To quick soak beans, place beans in large saucepan; cover with water. Bring to a boil over high heat. Boil 2 minutes. Remove from heat; let soak, covered, 1 hour.) Drain beans; discard water.

3. Combine soaked beans, water, bacon, contents of seasoning packet and bay leaves in Dutch oven. Bring to a boil over high heat. Cover; reduce heat and simmer 1½ hours. Add barbecue sauce and simmer, uncovered, 1 hour or until beans are tender. Remove and discard bay leaves.

Makes 8 to 10 servings

Chili Barbecue Beans

1 jar Chili Barbecue Beans Mix
3 to 4 cups water
8 slices crisp-cooked bacon, crumbled
   or 8 ounces smoked sausage,
   sliced

1 to 1½ cups barbecue sauce

1. Remove seasoning packet and bay leaves from jar; set aside.

2. Place beans in large bowl; cover with water. Soak 6 to 8 hours or overnight. (To quick soak beans, place beans in large saucepan; cover with water. Bring to a boil over high heat. Boil 2 minutes. Remove from heat; let soak, covered, 1 hour.) Drain beans; discard water.

3. Combine soaked beans, water, bacon, contents of seasoning packet and bay leaves in Dutch oven. Bring to a boil over high heat. Cover; reduce heat and simmer 1½ hours. Add barbecue sauce and simmer, uncovered, 1 hour or until beans are tender. Remove and discard bay leaves.

Makes 8 to 10 servings

Chili Barbecue Beans

1 jar Chili Barbecue Beans Mix
3 to 4 cups water
8 slices crisp-cooked bacon, crumbled
    or 8 ounces smoked sausage,
    sliced

1 to 1½ cups barbecue sauce

1. Remove seasoning packet and bay leaves from jar; set aside.

2. Place beans in large bowl; cover with water. Soak 6 to 8 hours or overnight. (To quick soak beans, place beans in large saucepan; cover with water. Bring to a boil over high heat. Boil 2 minutes. Remove from heat; let soak, covered, 1 hour.) Drain beans; discard water.

3. Combine soaked beans, water, bacon, contents of seasoning packet and bay leaves in Dutch oven. Bring to a boil over high heat. Cover; reduce heat and simmer 1½ hours. Add barbecue sauce and simmer, uncovered, 1 hour or until beans are tender. Remove and discard bay leaves. *Makes 8 to 10 servings*

Chili Barbecue Beans

1 jar Chili Barbecue Beans Mix
3 to 4 cups water
8 slices crisp-cooked bacon, crumbled
    or 8 ounces smoked sausage,
    sliced

1 to 1½ cups barbecue sauce

1. Remove seasoning packet and bay leaves from jar; set aside.

2. Place beans in large bowl; cover with water. Soak 6 to 8 hours or overnight. (To quick soak beans, place beans in large saucepan; cover with water. Bring to a boil over high heat. Boil 2 minutes. Remove from heat; let soak, covered, 1 hour.) Drain beans; discard water.

3. Combine soaked beans, water, bacon, contents of seasoning packet and bay leaves in Dutch oven. Bring to a boil over high heat. Cover; reduce heat and simmer 1½ hours. Add barbecue sauce and simmer, uncovered, 1 hour or until beans are tender. Remove and discard bay leaves. *Makes 8 to 10 servings*

Chili Barbecue Beans

1 jar Chili Barbecue Beans Mix
3 to 4 cups water
8 slices crisp-cooked bacon, crumbled
    or 8 ounces smoked sausage,
    sliced

1 to 1½ cups barbecue sauce

1. Remove seasoning packet and bay leaves from jar; set aside.

2. Place beans in large bowl; cover with water. Soak 6 to 8 hours or overnight. (To quick soak beans, place beans in large saucepan; cover with water. Bring to a boil over high heat. Boil 2 minutes. Remove from heat; let soak, covered, 1 hour.) Drain beans; discard water.

3. Combine soaked beans, water, bacon, contents of seasoning packet and bay leaves in Dutch oven. Bring to a boil over high heat. Cover; reduce heat and simmer 1½ hours. Add barbecue sauce and simmer, uncovered, 1 hour or until beans are tender. Remove and discard bay leaves. *Makes 8 to 10 servings*

Bean Dip for a Crowd Mix

1½ cups dried black beans
1½ cups dried pinto beans
2 bay leaves
1 package (about 1¼ ounces) hot taco seasoning mix
2 tablespoons dried minced onion
1 tablespoon dried parsley flakes
3 chicken bouillon cubes, unwrapped

1. Layer black beans and pinto beans in 1-quart food storage jar with tight-fitting lid. Slide bay leaves down side of jar. Place taco seasoning, onion, parsley and bouillon cubes in small food storage bag. Close with twist tie and cut off top of bag. Place bag on top of beans. Close jar.

2. Cover top of jar with fabric; attach gift tag with raffia or ribbon.

Makes one 1-quart jar

Gift Idea: Assemble a gift basket with a jar of Bean Dip for a Crowd Mix, a jar of salsa, taco seasoning, fresh limes and a bag of tortilla chips. For the holidays, use red and green tortilla chips.

Bean Dip for a Crowd

1 jar Bean Dip for a Crowd Mix
5 to 6 cups water
1 jar (16 ounces) thick and chunky salsa (medium or hot)
2 tablespoons lime juice

1. Remove seasoning packet and bay leaves from jar; set aside. Place beans in large bowl; cover with water. Soak 6 to 8 hours or overnight. (To quick soak beans, place beans in large saucepan; cover with water. Bring to a boil over high heat. Boil 2 minutes. Remove from heat; let soak, covered, 1 hour.) Drain beans; discard water.

2. Combine soaked beans, water, contents of seasoning packet and bay leaves in slow cooker. Cover and cook on LOW 9 to 10 hours. Remove and discard bay leaves. Ladle ½ hot bean mixture into food processor. Add salsa and lime juice. Cover and process until smooth. Return puréed dip to slow cooker; stir to combine.

Makes 6 cups dip

Conventional Method: Simmer bean mixture in step 2 in Dutch oven, partially covered, 2½ hours or until beans are tender.

Bean Dip for a Crowd

1 jar Bean Dip for a Crowd Mix
5 to 6 cups water

1 jar(16 ounces) thick and chunky
salsa (medium or hot)
2 tablespoons lime juice

1. Remove seasoning packet and bay leaves from jar; set aside. Place beans in large bowl; cover with water. Soak 6 to 8 hours or overnight. (To quick soak beans, place beans in large saucepan; cover with water. Bring to a boil over high heat. Boil 2 minutes. Remove from heat; let soak, covered, 1 hour.) Drain beans; discard water.

2. Combine soaked beans, water, contents of seasoning packet and bay leaves in slow cooker. Cover and cook on LOW 9 to 10 hours. Remove and discard bay leaves. Ladle ½ hot bean mixture into food processor. Add salsa and lime juice. Cover; process until smooth. Return puréed dip to slow cooker; stir to combine. *Makes 6 cups dip*

Conventional Method: Simmer bean mixture in step 2 in Dutch oven, partially covered, 2½ hours or until beans are tender.

Bean Dip for a Crowd

1 jar Bean Dip for a Crowd Mix
5 to 6 cups water

1 jar(16 ounces) thick and chunky
salsa (medium or hot)
2 tablespoons lime juice

1. Remove seasoning packet and bay leaves from jar; set aside. Place beans in large bowl; cover with water. Soak 6 to 8 hours or overnight. (To quick soak beans, place beans in large saucepan; cover with water. Bring to a boil over high heat. Boil 2 minutes. Remove from heat; let soak, covered, 1 hour.) Drain beans; discard water.

2. Combine soaked beans, water, contents of seasoning packet and bay leaves in slow cooker. Cover and cook on LOW 9 to 10 hours. Remove and discard bay leaves. Ladle ½ hot bean mixture into food processor. Add salsa and lime juice. Cover; process until smooth. Return puréed dip to slow cooker; stir to combine. *Makes 6 cups dip*

Conventional Method: Simmer bean mixture in step 2 in Dutch oven, partially covered, 2½ hours or until beans are tender.

Bean Dip for a Crowd

1 jar Bean Dip for a Crowd Mix
5 to 6 cups water

1 jar(16 ounces) thick and chunky
salsa (medium or hot)
2 tablespoons lime juice

1. Remove seasoning packet and bay leaves from jar; set aside. Place beans in large bowl; cover with water. Soak 6 to 8 hours or overnight. (To quick soak beans, place beans in large saucepan; cover with water. Bring to a boil over high heat. Boil 2 minutes. Remove from heat; let soak, covered, 1 hour.) Drain beans; discard water.

2. Combine soaked beans, water, contents of seasoning packet and bay leaves in slow cooker. Cover and cook on LOW 9 to 10 hours. Remove and discard bay leaves. Ladle ½ hot bean mixture into food processor. Add salsa and lime juice. Cover; process until smooth. Return puréed dip to slow cooker; stir to combine. *Makes 6 cups dip*

Conventional Method: Simmer bean mixture in step 2 in Dutch oven, partially covered, 2½ hours or until beans are tender.

Bean Dip for a Crowd

1 jar Bean Dip for a Crowd Mix	1 jar(16 ounces) thick and chunky
5 to 6 cups water	salsa (medium or hot)
	2 tablespoons lime juice

1. Remove seasoning packet and bay leaves from jar; set aside. Place beans in large bowl; cover with water. Soak 6 to 8 hours or overnight. (To quick soak beans, place beans in large saucepan; cover with water. Bring to a boil over high heat. Boil 2 minutes. Remove from heat; let soak, covered, 1 hour.) Drain beans; discard water.

2. Combine soaked beans, water, contents of seasoning packet and bay leaves in slow cooker. Cover and cook on LOW 9 to 10 hours. Remove and discard bay leaves. Ladle ½ hot bean mixture into food processor. Add salsa and lime juice. Cover; process until smooth. Return puréed dip to slow cooker; stir to combine.   *Makes 6 cups dip*

Conventional Method: Simmer bean mixture in step 2 in Dutch oven, partially covered, 2½ hours or until beans are tender.

Bean Dip for a Crowd

1 jar Bean Dip for a Crowd Mix	1 jar(16 ounces) thick and chunky
5 to 6 cups water	salsa (medium or hot)
	2 tablespoons lime juice

1. Remove seasoning packet and bay leaves from jar; set aside. Place beans in large bowl; cover with water. Soak 6 to 8 hours or overnight. (To quick soak beans, place beans in large saucepan; cover with water. Bring to a boil over high heat. Boil 2 minutes. Remove from heat; let soak, covered, 1 hour.) Drain beans; discard water.

2. Combine soaked beans, water, contents of seasoning packet and bay leaves in slow cooker. Cover and cook on LOW 9 to 10 hours. Remove and discard bay leaves. Ladle ½ hot bean mixture into food processor. Add salsa and lime juice. Cover; process until smooth. Return puréed dip to slow cooker; stir to combine.   *Makes 6 cups dip*

Conventional Method: Simmer bean mixture in step 2 in Dutch oven, partially covered, 2½ hours or until beans are tender.

Bean Dip for a Crowd

1 jar Bean Dip for a Crowd Mix	1 jar(16 ounces) thick and chunky
5 to 6 cups water	salsa (medium or hot)
	2 tablespoons lime juice

1. Remove seasoning packet and bay leaves from jar; set aside. Place beans in large bowl; cover with water. Soak 6 to 8 hours or overnight. (To quick soak beans, place beans in large saucepan; cover with water. Bring to a boil over high heat. Boil 2 minutes. Remove from heat; let soak, covered, 1 hour.) Drain beans; discard water.

2. Combine soaked beans, water, contents of seasoning packet and bay leaves in slow cooker. Cover and cook on LOW 9 to 10 hours. Remove and discard bay leaves. Ladle ½ hot bean mixture into food processor. Add salsa and lime juice. Cover; process until smooth. Return puréed dip to slow cooker; stir to combine.   *Makes 6 cups dip*

Conventional Method: Simmer bean mixture in step 2 in Dutch oven, partially covered, 2½ hours or until beans are tender.

Brown Rice with Porcini Mushrooms Mix

1 cup uncooked brown rice
6 sun-dried tomato halves, cut into pieces
1 tablespoon dried minced onion
1 tablespoon beef or vegetable bouillon granules
1 tablespoon dried chives
½ teaspoon dried minced garlic
¼ teaspoon dried thyme leaves
¼ teaspoon black pepper
½ cup dried porcini mushrooms
¼ cup grated Parmesan cheese

1. Layer ½ cup rice, sun-dried tomatoes, onion, bouillon granules, chives, garlic, thyme, pepper, remaining ½ cup rice and mushrooms in 1-pint food storage jar with tight-fitting lid. Place cheese in small food storage bag. Close with twist tie and cut off top of bag. Place on top of mushrooms. Close jar.

2. Cover top of jar with fabric; attach gift tag with raffia or ribbon.

Makes one 1-pint jar

Brown Rice with Porcini Mushrooms

    1 jar Brown Rice with Porcini Mushrooms Mix
2½ cups water
    1 tablespoon butter

1. Remove cheese packet from jar. Set aside.

2. Combine water, butter and remaining contents of jar in large saucepan. Bring to a boil over high heat. Cover; reduce heat and simmer 55 to 60 minutes or until rice is tender. Stir in Parmesan cheese.   *Makes 4 servings*

Brown Rice with Porcini Mushrooms

**1 jar Brown Rice with Porcini
  Mushrooms Mix**

**2½ cups water
1 tablespoon butter**

1. Remove cheese packet from jar. Set aside.

2. Combine water, butter and remaining contents of jar in large saucepan. Bring to a boil over high heat. Cover; reduce heat and simmer 55 to 60 minutes or until rice is tender. Stir in Parmesan cheese.

Makes 4 servings

Brown Rice with Porcini Mushrooms

**1 jar Brown Rice with Porcini
  Mushrooms Mix**

**2½ cups water
1 tablespoon butter**

1. Remove cheese packet from jar. Set aside.

2. Combine water, butter and remaining contents of jar in large saucepan. Bring to a boil over high heat. Cover; reduce heat and simmer 55 to 60 minutes or until rice is tender. Stir in Parmesan cheese.

Makes 4 servings

Brown Rice with Porcini Mushrooms

**1 jar Brown Rice with Porcini
  Mushrooms Mix**

**2½ cups water
1 tablespoon butter**

1. Remove cheese packet from jar. Set aside.

2. Combine water, butter and remaining contents of jar in large saucepan. Bring to a boil over high heat. Cover; reduce heat and simmer 55 to 60 minutes or until rice is tender. Stir in Parmesan cheese.

Makes 4 servings

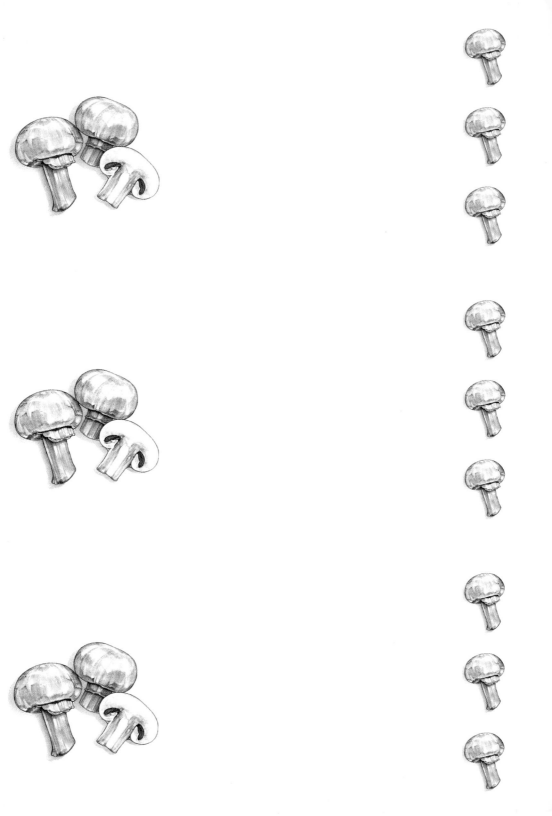

Brown Rice with Porcini Mushrooms

1 jar Brown Rice with Porcini
   Mushrooms Mix

2½ cups water
1 tablespoon butter

1. Remove cheese packet from jar. Set aside.

2. Combine water, butter and remaining contents of jar in large saucepan. Bring to a boil over high heat. Cover; reduce heat and simmer 55 to 60 minutes or until rice is tender. Stir in Parmesan cheese.

Makes 4 servings

Brown Rice with Porcini Mushrooms

1 jar Brown Rice with Porcini
   Mushrooms Mix

2½ cups water
1 tablespoon butter

1. Remove cheese packet from jar. Set aside.

2. Combine water, butter and remaining contents of jar in large saucepan. Bring to a boil over high heat. Cover; reduce heat and simmer 55 to 60 minutes or until rice is tender. Stir in Parmesan cheese.

Makes 4 servings

Brown Rice with Porcini Mushrooms

1 jar Brown Rice with Porcini
   Mushrooms Mix

2½ cups water
1 tablespoon butter

1. Remove cheese packet from jar. Set aside.

2. Combine water, butter and remaining contents of jar in large saucepan. Bring to a boil over high heat. Cover; reduce heat and simmer 55 to 60 minutes or until rice is tender. Stir in Parmesan cheese.

Makes 4 servings

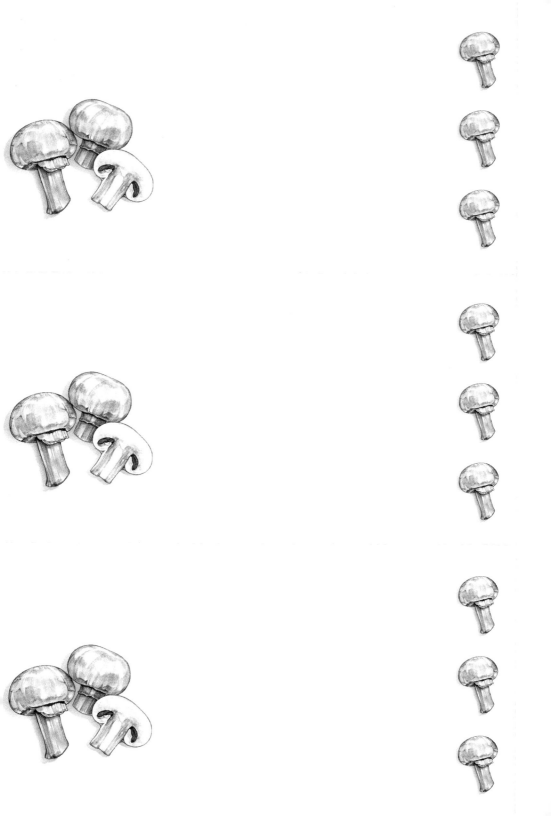

Fruited Rice Mix

½ cup uncooked brown rice
2 tablespoons dried minced onion
1 tablespoon dried parsley flakes
2 teaspoons chicken bouillon granules
2 teaspoons firmly packed brown sugar
½ teaspoon dried thyme leaves
¼ teaspoon black pepper
⅛ teaspoon ground red pepper
½ cup uncooked wild rice
¼ cup chopped dried apricots
¼ cup chopped dried cranberries or cherries
¼ cup raisins or currants

1. Layer brown rice, onion, parsley, bouillon granules, brown sugar, thyme, black pepper, red pepper and wild rice in 1-pint food storage jar with tight-fitting lid. Combine apricots, cranberries and raisins in small food storage bag. Close with twist tie and cut off top of bag. Place bag on top of rice. Close jar.

2. Cover top of jar with fabric; attach gift tag with raffia or ribbon.

Makes one 1-pint jar

Fruited Rice

1 jar Fruited Rice Mix
2¼ cups water
1 tablespoon butter
¼ to ½ cup orange juice

1. Remove dried fruit packet from jar; set aside.

2. Combine water, butter and remaining contents of jar in large saucepan. Bring to a boil over high heat. Cover; reduce heat and simmer 45 to 50 minutes or until rice is almost tender.

3. Stir in orange juice and contents of dried fruit packet. Simmer, uncovered, 15 minutes or until rice is tender.   *Makes 4 servings*

Fruited Rice

1 jar Fruited Rice Mix
2¼ cups water

1 tablespoon butter
¼ to ½ cup orange juice

1. Remove dried fruit packet from jar; set aside.

2. Combine water, butter and remaining contents of jar in large saucepan. Bring to a boil over high heat. Cover; reduce heat and simmer 45 to 50 minutes or until rice is almost tender.

3. Stir in orange juice and contents of dried fruit packet. Simmer, uncovered, 15 minutes or until rice is tender. *Makes 4 servings*

Fruited Rice

1 jar Fruited Rice Mix
2¼ cups water

1 tablespoon butter
¼ to ½ cup orange juice

1. Remove dried fruit packet from jar; set aside.

2. Combine water, butter and remaining contents of jar in large saucepan. Bring to a boil over high heat. Cover; reduce heat and simmer 45 to 50 minutes or until rice is almost tender.

3. Stir in orange juice and contents of dried fruit packet. Simmer, uncovered, 15 minutes or until rice is tender. *Makes 4 servings*

Fruited Rice

1 jar Fruited Rice Mix
2¼ cups water

1 tablespoon butter
¼ to ½ cup orange juice

1. Remove dried fruit packet from jar; set aside.

2. Combine water, butter and remaining contents of jar in large saucepan. Bring to a boil over high heat. Cover; reduce heat and simmer 45 to 50 minutes or until rice is almost tender.

3. Stir in orange juice and contents of dried fruit packet. Simmer, uncovered, 15 minutes or until rice is tender. *Makes 4 servings*

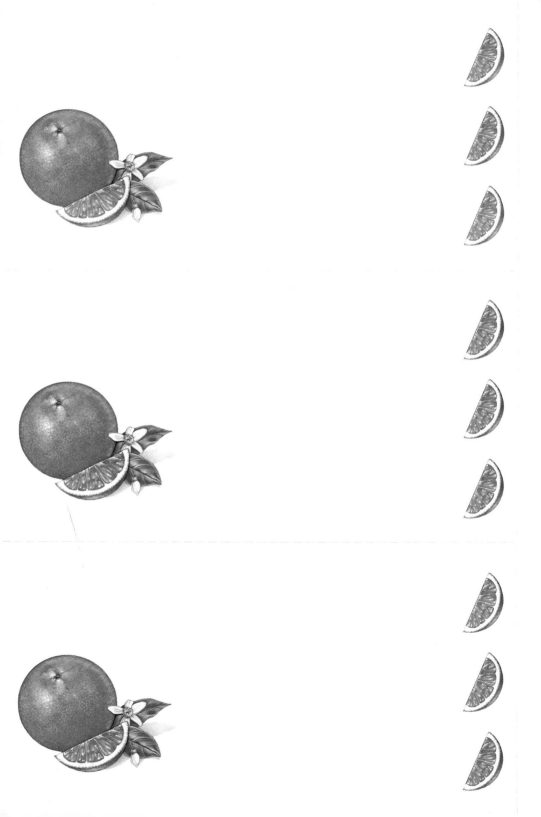

Fruited Rice

1 jar Fruited Rice Mix
2¼ cups water

1 tablespoon butter
¼ to ½ cup orange juice

1. Remove dried fruit packet from jar; set aside.

2. Combine water, butter and remaining contents of jar in large saucepan. Bring to a boil over high heat. Cover; reduce heat and simmer 45 to 50 minutes or until rice is almost tender.

3. Stir in orange juice and contents of dried fruit packet. Simmer, uncovered, 15 minutes or until rice is tender.

Makes 4 servings

Fruited Rice

1 jar Fruited Rice Mix
2¼ cups water

1 tablespoon butter
¼ to ½ cup orange juice

1. Remove dried fruit packet from jar; set aside.

2. Combine water, butter and remaining contents of jar in large saucepan. Bring to a boil over high heat. Cover; reduce heat and simmer 45 to 50 minutes or until rice is almost tender.

3. Stir in orange juice and contents of dried fruit packet. Simmer, uncovered, 15 minutes or until rice is tender.

Makes 4 servings

Fruited Rice

1 jar Fruited Rice Mix
2¼ cups water

1 tablespoon butter
¼ to ½ cup orange juice

1. Remove dried fruit packet from jar; set aside.

2. Combine water, butter and remaining contents of jar in large saucepan. Bring to a boil over high heat. Cover; reduce heat and simmer 45 to 50 minutes or until rice is almost tender.

3. Stir in orange juice and contents of dried fruit packet. Simmer, uncovered, 15 minutes or until rice is tender.

Makes 4 servings

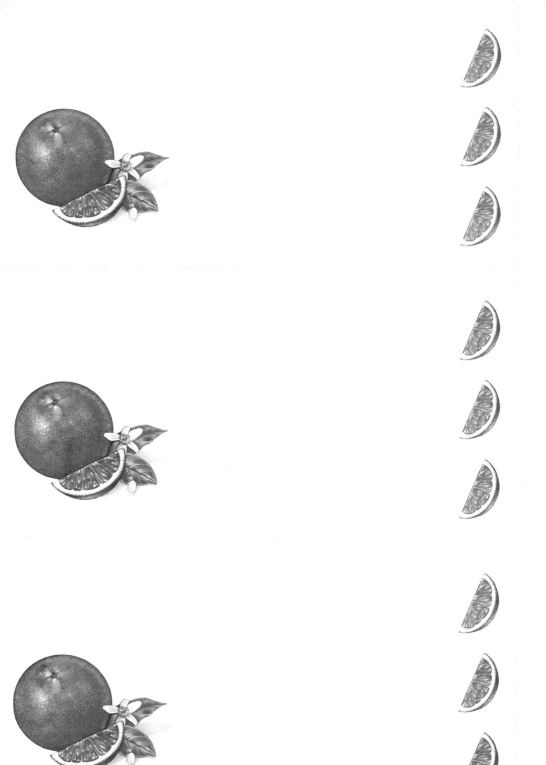

Nutty Orzo and Rice Pilaf Mix

¾ cup uncooked orzo pasta
 3 tablespoons dried vegetable flakes
 2 teaspoons chicken bouillon granules
 ½ teaspoon dried thyme leaves
 ¼ teaspoon black pepper
 ½ cup uncooked instant brown rice
 ½ cup pecan pieces

1. Layer orzo, vegetable flakes, bouillon granules, thyme, pepper and rice in 1-pint food storage jar with tight-fitting lid. Place pecans in small food storage bag. Close with twist tie and cut off top of bag. Place bag on top of rice. Close jar.

2. Cover top of jar with fabric; attach gift tag with raffia or ribbon.

Makes one 1-pint jar

Nutty Orzo and Rice Pilaf

    1 jar Nutty Orzo and Rice Pilaf Mix
    2 cups water
    1 tablespoon butter

1. Remove pecan packet from jar; set aside.

2. Combine water, butter and contents of jar in large saucepan. Bring to a boil over high heat. Cover; reduce heat and simmer 10 to 15 minutes or until orzo is tender.

3. While pilaf is cooking, toast pecans on baking sheet in preheated 350°F oven for 5 to 8 minutes or until nuts just begin to darken.

4. Stir pecans into pilaf. Cook, uncovered, 2 to 3 minutes or until heated through.   *Makes 4 to 5 servings*

Variations: Add 1 cup cooked peas and carrots *or* ½ cup drained canned sliced mushrooms in step 4. Heat through.

Nutty Orzo and Rice Pilaf

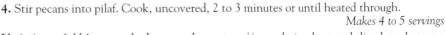

1 jar Nutty Orzo and Rice Pilaf Mix
2 cups water
1 tablespoon butter

1. Remove pecan packet from jar; set aside.

2. Combine water, butter and contents of jar in large saucepan. Bring to a boil over high heat. Cover; reduce heat and simmer 10 to 15 minutes or until orzo is tender.

3. While pilaf is cooking, toast pecans on baking sheet in preheated 350°F oven for 5 to 8 minutes or until nuts just begin to darken.

4. Stir pecans into pilaf. Cook, uncovered, 2 to 3 minutes or until heated through.

Makes 4 to 5 servings

Variations: Add 1 cup cooked peas and carrots *or* ½ cup drained canned sliced mushrooms in step 4. Heat through.

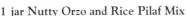

Nutty Orzo and Rice Pilaf

1 jar Nutty Orzo and Rice Pilaf Mix
2 cups water
1 tablespoon butter

1. Remove pecan packet from jar; set aside.

2. Combine water, butter and contents of jar in large saucepan. Bring to a boil over high heat. Cover; reduce heat and simmer 10 to 15 minutes or until orzo is tender.

3. While pilaf is cooking, toast pecans on baking sheet in preheated 350°F oven for 5 to 8 minutes or until nuts just begin to darken.

4. Stir pecans into pilaf. Cook, uncovered, 2 to 3 minutes or until heated through.

Makes 4 to 5 servings

Variations: Add 1 cup cooked peas and carrots *or* ½ cup drained canned sliced mushrooms in step 4. Heat through.

Nutty Orzo and Rice Pilaf

1 jar Nutty Orzo and Rice Pilaf Mix
2 cups water
1 tablespoon butter

1. Remove pecan packet from jar; set aside.

2. Combine water, butter and contents of jar in large saucepan. Bring to a boil over high heat. Cover; reduce heat and simmer 10 to 15 minutes or until orzo is tender.

3. While pilaf is cooking, toast pecans on baking sheet in preheated 350°F oven for 5 to 8 minutes or until nuts just begin to darken.

4. Stir pecans into pilaf. Cook, uncovered, 2 to 3 minutes or until heated through.

Makes 4 to 5 servings

Variations: Add 1 cup cooked peas and carrots *or* ½ cup drained canned sliced mushrooms in step 4. Heat through.

Nutty Orzo and Rice Pilaf

1 jar Nutty Orzo and Rice Pilaf Mix
2 cups water
1 tablespoon butter

1. Remove pecan packet from jar; set aside.

2. Combine water, butter and contents of jar in large saucepan. Bring to a boil over high heat. Cover; reduce heat and simmer 10 to 15 minutes or until orzo is tender.

3. While pilaf is cooking, toast pecans on baking sheet in preheated 350°F oven for 5 to 8 minutes or until nuts just begin to darken.

4. Stir pecans into pilaf. Cook, uncovered, 2 to 3 minutes or until heated through.

Makes 4 to 5 servings

Variations: Add 1 cup cooked peas and carrots *or* ½ cup drained canned sliced mushrooms in step 4. Heat through.

Nutty Orzo and Rice Pilaf

1 jar Nutty Orzo and Rice Pilaf Mix
2 cups water
1 tablespoon butter

1. Remove pecan packet from jar; set aside.

2. Combine water, butter and contents of jar in large saucepan. Bring to a boil over high heat. Cover; reduce heat and simmer 10 to 15 minutes or until orzo is tender.

3. While pilaf is cooking, toast pecans on baking sheet in preheated 350°F oven for 5 to 8 minutes or until nuts just begin to darken.

4. Stir pecans into pilaf. Cook, uncovered, 2 to 3 minutes or until heated through.

Makes 4 to 5 servings

Variations: Add 1 cup cooked peas and carrots *or* ½ cup drained canned sliced mushrooms in step 4. Heat through.

Nutty Orzo and Rice Pilaf

1 jar Nutty Orzo and Rice Pilaf Mix
2 cups water
1 tablespoon butter

1. Remove pecan packet from jar; set aside.

2. Combine water, butter and contents of jar in large saucepan. Bring to a boil over high heat. Cover; reduce heat and simmer 10 to 15 minutes or until orzo is tender.

3. While pilaf is cooking, toast pecans on baking sheet in preheated 350°F oven for 5 to 8 minutes or until nuts just begin to darken.

4. Stir pecans into pilaf. Cook, uncovered, 2 to 3 minutes or until heated through.

Makes 4 to 5 servings

Variations: Add 1 cup cooked peas and carrots *or* ½ cup drained canned sliced mushrooms in step 4. Heat through.

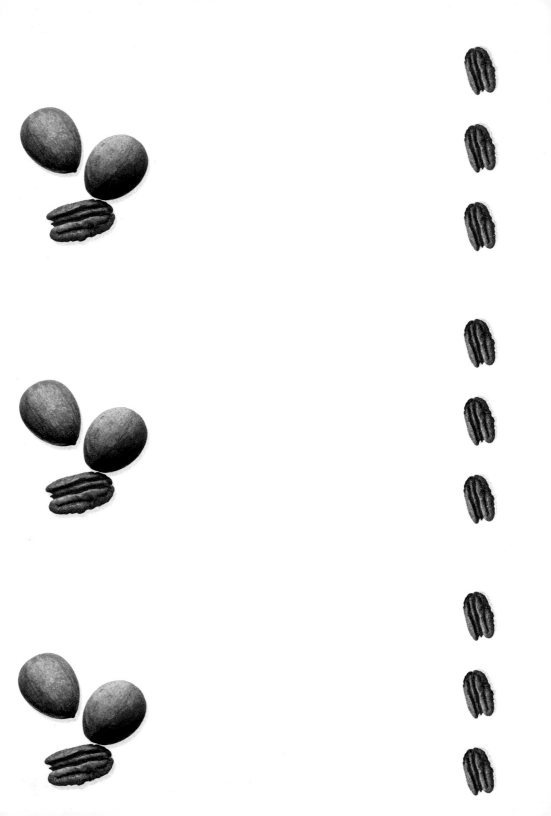

Penne with Artichokes Mix

3 cups uncooked tricolor penne or rotini pasta
¼ cup sun-dried tomato halves*
¼ cup grated Romano cheese
1 tablespoon dried parsley flakes
½ teaspoon dried minced garlic
⅛ to ¼ teaspoon red pepper flakes
¼ teaspoon black pepper

*Sun-dried tomato halves may be cut into pieces.

1. Layer 1½ cups penne, sun-dried tomatoes and remaining 1½ cups penne in 1-quart food storage jar with tight-fitting lid. Place Romano cheese, parsley, garlic, red pepper flakes and black pepper into small food storage bag. Close bag with twist tie and cut off top of bag. Place on top of penne. Close jar.

2. Cover top of jar with fabric; attach gift tag with raffia or ribbon.

Makes one 1-quart jar

Penne with Artichokes

1 jar Penne with Artichokes Mix
4 cups water
½ teaspoon salt
1 can (14½ ounces) quartered artichokes, drained
1 tablespoon butter
1 teaspoon olive oil
½ cup roasted red pepper strips

1. Remove cheese packet from jar; set aside.

2. Place water, salt and remaining contents of jar in large saucepan. Bring to a boil and boil 12 to 15 minutes or until pasta is tender. Drain and return to pan.

3. Stir in artichokes, butter, olive oil, red pepper strips and contents of cheese packet. Cover and cook over medium heat 3 to 5 minutes until hot. *Makes 4 to 5 servings*

Penne with Artichokes

1 jar Penne with Artichokes Mix
4 cups water
½ teaspoon salt
1 can (14½ ounces) quartered
    artichokes, drained

1 tablespoon butter
1 teaspoon olive oil
½ cup roasted red pepper strips

1. Remove cheese packet from jar; set aside.

2. Place water, salt and remaining contents of jar in large saucepan. Bring to a boil and boil 12 to 15 minutes or until pasta is tender. Drain pasta and return to pan.

3. Stir in artichokes, butter, olive oil, red pepper strips and contents of cheese packet. Cover and cook over medium heat 3 to 5 minutes until hot. *Makes 4 to 5 servings*

Penne with Artichokes

1 jar Penne with Artichokes Mix
4 cups water
½ teaspoon salt
1 can (14½ ounces) quartered
    artichokes, drained

1 tablespoon butter
1 teaspoon olive oil
½ cup roasted red pepper strips

1. Remove cheese packet from jar; set aside.

2. Place water, salt and remaining contents of jar in large saucepan. Bring to a boil and boil 12 to 15 minutes or until pasta is tender. Drain pasta and return to pan.

3. Stir in artichokes, butter, olive oil, red pepper strips and contents of cheese packet. Cover and cook over medium heat 3 to 5 minutes until hot. *Makes 4 to 5 servings*

Penne with Artichokes

1 jar Penne with Artichokes Mix
4 cups water
½ teaspoon salt
1 can (14½ ounces) quartered
    artichokes, drained

1 tablespoon butter
1 teaspoon olive oil
½ cup roasted red pepper strips

1. Remove cheese packet from jar; set aside.

2. Place water, salt and remaining contents of jar in large saucepan. Bring to a boil and boil 12 to 15 minutes or until pasta is tender. Drain pasta and return to pan.

3. Stir in artichokes, butter, olive oil, red pepper strips and contents of cheese packet. Cover and cook over medium heat 3 to 5 minutes until hot. *Makes 4 to 5 servings*

Quick & Easy Couscous Mix

1 cup uncooked couscous
¼ cup dried cranberries
¼ cup currants
2 tablespoons dried vegetable flakes
1 tablespoon dried minced onion
1 tablespoon dried parsley flakes
1 teaspoon chicken bouillon granules
¾ teaspoon curry powder
½ teaspoon salt
½ teaspoon black pepper
¼ teaspoon tumeric
¼ cup slivered almonds

1. Layer ½ cup couscous, cranberries, currants, vegetable flakes, onion, parsley, bouillon granules, curry powder, salt, pepper, tumeric and remaining ½ cup couscous in 1-pint food storage jar with tight-fitting lid. Place almonds in small food storage bag. Close with twist tie and cut off top of bag. Place bag on top of couscous. Close jar.
2. Cover top of jar with fabric; attach gift tag with raffia or ribbon.

Makes one 1-pint jar

Quick & Easy Couscous

1 jar Quick & Easy Couscous Mix
1½ cups water
1 tablespoon butter

1. Remove almond packet from jar; set aside.

2. Place water, butter and remaining contents of jar in a large saucepan. Bring to a boil. Remove pan from heat; cover and let stand 5 minutes.

3. Meanwhile, toast almonds. Spread nuts on shallow baking pan. Bake in preheated 350°F oven 5 to 8 minutes or until nuts are golden brown.

4. Fluff couscous with fork; stir in almonds.

Makes 4 to 5 servings

Quick & Easy Couscous

1 jar Quick & Easy Couscous Mix
1½ cups water
1 tablespoon butter

1. Remove almond packet from jar; set aside.

2. Place water, butter and remaining contents of jar in a large saucepan. Bring to a boil. Remove pan from heat; cover and let stand 5 minutes.

3. Meanwhile, toast almonds. Spread nuts on shallow baking pan. Bake in preheated 350°F oven 5 to 8 minutes or until nuts are golden brown.

4. Fluff couscous with fork; stir in almonds. *Makes 4 to 5 servings*

Quick & Easy Couscous

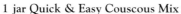

1 jar Quick & Easy Couscous Mix
1½ cups water
1 tablespoon butter

1. Remove almond packet from jar; set aside.

2. Place water, butter and remaining contents of jar in a large saucepan. Bring to a boil. Remove pan from heat; cover and let stand 5 minutes.

3. Meanwhile, toast almonds. Spread nuts on shallow baking pan. Bake in preheated 350°F oven 5 to 8 minutes or until nuts are golden brown.

4. Fluff couscous with fork; stir in almonds. *Makes 4 to 5 servings*

Quick & Easy Couscous

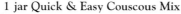

1 jar Quick & Easy Couscous Mix
1½ cups water
1 tablespoon butter

1. Remove almond packet from jar; set aside.

2. Place water, butter and remaining contents of jar in a large saucepan. Bring to a boil. Remove pan from heat; cover and let stand 5 minutes.

3. Meanwhile, toast almonds. Spread nuts on shallow baking pan. Bake in preheated 350°F oven 5 to 8 minutes or until nuts are golden brown.

4. Fluff couscous with fork; stir in almonds. *Makes 4 to 5 servings*

Quick & Easy Couscous

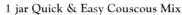

1 jar Quick & Easy Couscous Mix
1½ cups water
1 tablespoon butter

1. Remove almond packet from jar; set aside.

2. Place water, butter and remaining contents of jar in a large saucepan. Bring to a boil. Remove pan from heat; cover and let stand 5 minutes.

3. Meanwhile, toast almonds. Spread nuts on shallow baking pan. Bake in preheated 350°F oven 5 to 8 minutes or until nuts are golden brown.

4. Fluff couscous with fork; stir in almonds. *Makes 4 to 5 servings*

Quick & Easy Couscous

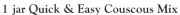

1 jar Quick & Easy Couscous Mix
1½ cups water
1 tablespoon butter

1. Remove almond packet from jar; set aside.

2. Place water, butter and remaining contents of jar in a large saucepan. Bring to a boil. Remove pan from heat; cover and let stand 5 minutes.

3. Meanwhile, toast almonds. Spread nuts on shallow baking pan. Bake in preheated 350°F oven 5 to 8 minutes or until nuts are golden brown.

4. Fluff couscous with fork; stir in almonds. *Makes 4 to 5 servings*

Quick & Easy Couscous

1 jar Quick & Easy Couscous Mix
1½ cups water
1 tablespoon butter

1. Remove almond packet from jar; set aside.

2. Place water, butter and remaining contents of jar in a large saucepan. Bring to a boil. Remove pan from heat; cover and let stand 5 minutes.

3. Meanwhile, toast almonds. Spread nuts on shallow baking pan. Bake in preheated 350°F oven 5 to 8 minutes or until nuts are golden brown.

4. Fluff couscous with fork; stir in almonds. *Makes 4 to 5 servings*

Crunchy Curried Snack Mix

2½ cups rice cereal squares
¾ cup walnut halves
¾ cup dried cherries or dried cranberries
2 tablespoons brown sugar
1½ teaspoons curry powder
¼ teaspoon ground cumin
¼ teaspoon salt

1. Layer 1¼ cups cereal, walnuts, cherries and remaining 1¼ cups cereal in 2-quart food storage jar with tight-fitting lid. Combine brown sugar, curry powder, cumin and salt in small food storage bag. Close with twist tie and cut off top of bag. Place bag on top of cereal. Close jar.

2. Cover top of jar with fabric; attach gift tag with raffia or ribbon.

Makes one 2-quart jar

Gift Idea: Assemble a jar of Crunchy Curried Snack Mix and a favorite beverage (wine, beer or soda) in a decorative gift basket or bag.

Crunchy Curried Snack Mix

1 jar Crunchy Curried Snack Mix
6 tablespoons butter

1. Remove seasoning packet from jar.

2. Melt butter in large skillet. Add contents of seasoning packet; mix well. Add remaining contents of jar; stir to coat. To crisp in slow cooker, spoon mixture into slow cooker. Cover and cook on LOW 3 hours. Remove cover; cook an additional 30 minutes. To crisp in oven, spread out mixture evenly on jelly-roll pan. Bake in preheated 250°F oven for 40 to 45 minutes or until crispy, stirring every 15 minutes. *Makes 6 cups snack mix*

Crunchy Curried Snack Mix

1 jar Crunchy Curried Snack Mix
6 tablespoons butter

1. Remove seasoning packet from jar.

2. Melt butter in large skillet. Add contents of seasoning packet; mix well. Add remaining contents of jar; stir to coat. To crisp in slow cooker, spoon mixture into slow cooker. Cover and cook on LOW 3 hours. Remove cover; cook an additional 30 minutes. To crisp in oven, spread out mixture evenly on jelly-roll pan. Bake in preheated 250°F oven for 40 to 45 minutes or until crispy, stirring every 15 minutes. *Makes 6 cups snack mix*

Crunchy Curried Snack Mix

1 jar Crunchy Curried Snack Mix
6 tablespoons butter

1. Remove seasoning packet from jar.

2. Melt butter in large skillet. Add contents of seasoning packet; mix well. Add remaining contents of jar; stir to coat. To crisp in slow cooker, spoon mixture into slow cooker. Cover and cook on LOW 3 hours. Remove cover; cook an additional 30 minutes. To crisp in oven, spread out mixture evenly on jelly-roll pan. Bake in preheated 250°F oven for 40 to 45 minutes or until crispy, stirring every 15 minutes. *Makes 6 cups snack mix*

Crunchy Curried Snack Mix

1 jar Crunchy Curried Snack Mix
6 tablespoons butter

1. Remove seasoning packet from jar.

2. Melt butter in large skillet. Add contents of seasoning packet; mix well. Add remaining contents of jar; stir to coat. To crisp in slow cooker, spoon mixture into slow cooker. Cover and cook on LOW 3 hours. Remove cover; cook an additional 30 minutes. To crisp in oven, spread out mixture evenly on jelly-roll pan. Bake in preheated 250°F oven for 40 to 45 minutes or until crispy, stirring every 15 minutes. *Makes 6 cups snack mix*

Crunchy Curried Snack Mix

1 jar Crunchy Curried Snack Mix
6 tablespoons butter

1. Remove seasoning packet from jar.

2. Melt butter in large skillet. Add contents of seasoning packet; mix well. Add remaining contents of jar; stir to coat. To crisp in slow cooker, spoon mixture into slow cooker. Cover and cook on LOW 3 hours. Remove cover; cook an additional 30 minutes. To crisp in oven, spread out mixture evenly on jelly-roll pan. Bake in preheated 250°F oven for 40 to 45 minutes or until crispy, stirring every 15 minutes. *Makes 6 cups snack mix*

Crunchy Curried Snack Mix

1 jar Crunchy Curried Snack Mix
6 tablespoons butter

1. Remove seasoning packet from jar.

2. Melt butter in large skillet. Add contents of seasoning packet; mix well. Add remaining contents of jar; stir to coat. To crisp in slow cooker, spoon mixture into slow cooker. Cover and cook on LOW 3 hours. Remove cover; cook an additional 30 minutes. To crisp in oven, spread out mixture evenly on jelly-roll pan. Bake in preheated 250°F oven for 40 to 45 minutes or until crispy, stirring every 15 minutes. *Makes 6 cups snack mix*

Crunchy Curried Snack Mix

1 jar Crunchy Curried Snack Mix
6 tablespoons butter

1. Remove seasoning packet from jar.

2. Melt butter in large skillet. Add contents of seasoning packet; mix well. Add remaining contents of jar; stir to coat. To crisp in slow cooker, spoon mixture into slow cooker. Cover and cook on LOW 3 hours. Remove cover; cook an additional 30 minutes. To crisp in oven, spread out mixture evenly on jelly-roll pan. Bake in preheated 250°F oven for 40 to 45 minutes or until crispy, stirring every 15 minutes. *Makes 6 cups snack mix*

Sweet & Spicy Snack Mix

    3 cups popped corn
  2½ cups miniature or holiday-shaped pretzels
    1 cup pecan halves or pistachios
  ⅓ cup packed brown sugar
  ½ teaspoon ground cinnamon
  ¼ teaspoon ground red pepper

1. Layer popped corn, pretzels and pecans in any order in 2-quart food storage jar with tight-fitting lid. Place brown sugar, cinnamon and red pepper in small food storage bag. Close bag with twist tie. Cut off top of bag. Put in jar; close.

2. Cover top of jar with fabric; attach gift tag with raffia or ribbon.

Makes one 2-quart jar

Sweet & Spicy Snack Mix

1 jar Sweet & Spicy Snack Mix
¼ cup butter

1. Remove seasoning packet from jar. Place butter and contents of seasoning packet in 4-quart microwavable bowl. Microwave at HIGH 1½ minutes or until bubbly. Remove from oven; stir in remaining contents of jar; mixing well. Microwave at HIGH 1 to 2 minutes. Remove and stir to coat mixture evenly. Cool completely.

Makes 6 cups snack mix

Sweet & Spicy Snack Mix

----

1 jar Sweet & Spicy Snack Mix
¼ cup butter

1. Remove seasoning packet from jar. Place butter and contents of seasoning packet in 4-quart microwavable bowl. Microwave at HIGH 1½ minutes or until bubbly. Remove from oven; stir in remaining contents of jar; mixing well. Microwave at HIGH 1 to 2 minutes. Remove and stir to coat mixture evenly. Cool completely.

Makes 6 cups snack mix

Sweet & Spicy Snack Mix

----

1 jar Sweet & Spicy Snack Mix
¼ cup butter

1. Remove seasoning packet from jar. Place butter and contents of seasoning packet in 4-quart microwavable bowl. Microwave at HIGH 1½ minutes or until bubbly. Remove from oven; stir in remaining contents of jar; mixing well. Microwave at HIGH 1 to 2 minutes. Remove and stir to coat mixture evenly. Cool completely.

Makes 6 cups snack mix

Sweet & Spicy Snack Mix

----

1 jar Sweet & Spicy Snack Mix
¼ cup butter

1. Remove seasoning packet from jar. Place butter and contents of seasoning packet in 4-quart microwavable bowl. Microwave at HIGH 1½ minutes or until bubbly. Remove from oven; stir in remaining contents of jar; mixing well. Microwave at HIGH 1 to 2 minutes. Remove and stir to coat mixture evenly. Cool completely.

Makes 6 cups snack mix

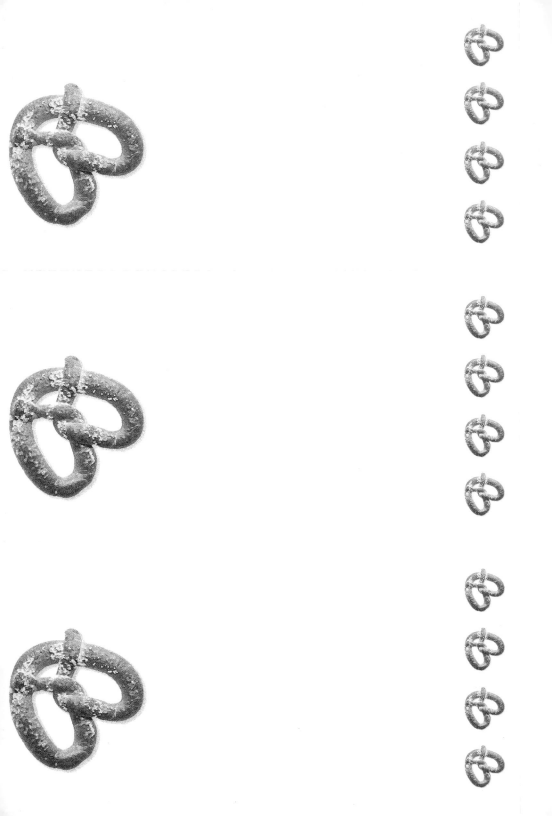

Sweet & Spicy Snack Mix

1 jar Sweet & Spicy Snack Mix
¼ cup butter

1. Remove seasoning packet from jar. Place butter and contents of seasoning packet in 4-quart microwavable bowl. Microwave at HIGH 1½ minutes or until bubbly. Remove from oven; stir in remaining contents of jar; mixing well. Microwave at HIGH 1 to 2 minutes. Remove and stir to coat mixture evenly. Cool completely.

Makes 6 cups snack mix

Sweet & Spicy Snack Mix

1 jar Sweet & Spicy Snack Mix
¼ cup butter

1. Remove seasoning packet from jar. Place butter and contents of seasoning packet in 4-quart microwavable bowl. Microwave at HIGH 1½ minutes or until bubbly. Remove from oven; stir in remaining contents of jar; mixing well. Microwave at HIGH 1 to 2 minutes. Remove and stir to coat mixture evenly. Cool completely.

Makes 6 cups snack mix

Sweet & Spicy Snack Mix

1 jar Sweet & Spicy Snack Mix
¼ cup butter

1. Remove seasoning packet from jar. Place butter and contents of seasoning packet in 4-quart microwavable bowl. Microwave at HIGH 1½ minutes or until bubbly. Remove from oven; stir in remaining contents of jar; mixing well. Microwave at HIGH 1 to 2 minutes. Remove and stir to coat mixture evenly. Cool completely.

Makes 6 cups snack mix

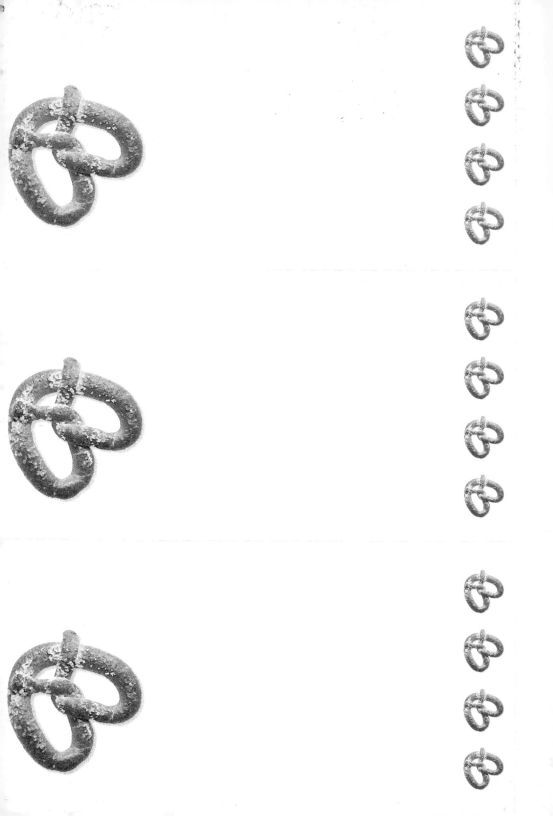